TURTLE MEAT

AND OTHER STORIES

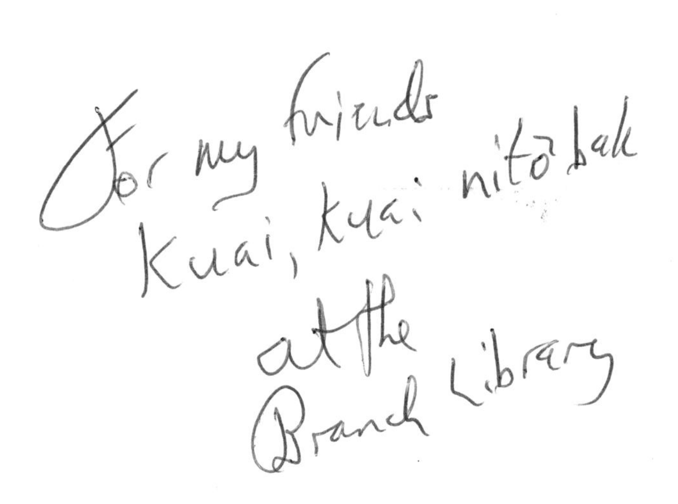

ALSO BY JOSEPH BRUCHAC:

NON FICTION:

Keepers of the Animals, co-author Michael Caduto (1991)
Keepers of the Earth, co-author Michael Caduto (1988)
Survival This Way: Interviews with American Indian Poets (1987)

STORYTELLING:

Native American Animal Stories (1992)
Thirteen Moons on Turtle's Back, co-author Jonathan London (1992)
Native American Stories from Keepers of the Earth (1991)
Hoop Snakes, Hide-Behinds & Side-Hill Winders, Adirondack Tall Tales (1991)
Return of the Sun: Native American Tales from the Eastern Woodlands (1989)
The Faithful Hunter and Other Abenaki Stories (1988)
Iroquois Stories: Heros and Heroines, Monsters and Magic (1985)
The Wind Eagle: Abenaki Stories (1985)

POETRY:

Translator's Son (1989)
Near the Mountains (1986)
Tracking (1985)

AUDIO CASSETTE TAPES:

Keepers of the Earth (1991)
The Boy Who Lived With The Bears (1990)
Gluskabe Stories (1990)
Iroquois Stories (1988)

TURTLE MEAT
AND OTHER STORIES

JOSEPH BRUCHAC

Illustrations by Murv Jacob

HOLY COW! PRESS • DULUTH, MINNESOTA • 1992

First Printing, 1992

Library of Congress Cataloging-in-Publication Data

Bruchac, Joseph
Turtle Meat and other stories / by Joseph Bruchac
p. cm.
ISBN 0-930100-48-4 (cloth) – ISBN 0-930100-49-2 (pbk.)
1. Saratoga Springs Region (N.Y.)—Fiction. 2. Indians of North America—New York (State)—Saratoga Springs Region—Fiction.
I. Title
PS3552.R794T87 1992
813' .54—dc20 92-54182
CIP

Publisher's Address:

Holy Cow! Press
Post Office Box 3170
Mount Royal Station
Duluth, Minnesota 55803

Distributor's Address:

The Talman Company
131 Spring Street
Suite 201E-N
New York, New York 10012

This project is supported, in part, by a grant from the National Endowment for the Arts in Washington, D.C., a Federal agency.

Table of Contents

For the old people whose voices have never left us.

The Ice-Hearts

It was the Moon of Long Nights when the Ice-Hearts came to us. They came down the long river which flows north to shores where the water is filled with salt and goes on without ending. Along the northern bank of that river they had walked and then, at a place where winter closed the lips of the stream, they crossed.

Ice was frozen to their faces, frozen in the hair that covered their faces. Their clothing was grey and hard, the color of flint. They carried long knives and big axes shiny as ice. And their hearts, it seemed, were made of ice, too, for they came down on our peaceful village and killed, the coldness of ice in their sky-colored eyes. They killed and stole food and then vanished back into the storm which seemed to have given them birth.

They were hard fighters, but not all of them got away. Two of them we caught among the small trees. One was tangled in some vines and the other stood by him, cutting him free. We circled them. They turned slowly from side to side as we circled. We could see then that it was not their skin which was hard as flint, so hard our arrows broke when they struck, but some kind of armor they were wearing. We knew of armor, for some of us wore armor when we fought, an armor made of hard pieces of wood. We moved closer . . . and one of them raised his axe up quickly, as if he meant to throw it. That was when Big Duck threw himself to the ground. He dropped just like a duck hit by an arrow and as he hit the ground he farted.

That was so funny that we all laughed. Eagle Circling, Eats Like A Bear, and even Big Duck himself as he lay there. Maybe those ice-hearted men were going to kill some of us, maybe we were going to kill them, but this was funny. And I, Fox Looking Around, I laughed the hardest, I think. But I kept my eye on the Ice-Hearts as I laughed. I was not ready to die laughing. But they were laughing, too! When Death has a hand on your shoulder you do strange things. Just as we laughed, they laughed, a laughter which took away the grimness and anger from their eyes. That was when we saw how young they were. And as they laughed we came up to them and took away their long knives and axes.

Two people had died when the Ice-Hearts came. One was an old man sleeping by the door of the longhouse. His nickname was Goes In The Corner because he always hated to go outside when winter came. Even though his wife was very stern with him, the part of the longhouse where they lived sometimes smelled of urine. The leader of the Ice-Hearts stuck his long knife right through the old man's stomach when he stood as they forced their way in through the door. Old Goes In The Corner shouted once and then fell, half in and half out the door. People woke up fast then. It seemed as if a Whirlwind had forced its way into the longhouse. Some people tried to get as far away from that door as they could. Others grabbed weapons and formed a half circle to face the invaders. Someone threw dry wood on the central fire and it blazed up, showing us the tall figures of strange men who looked like no people we had ever seen before. More of them forced their way in, standing shoulder to shoulder, until there were at least as many of them as there were of our fighting men facing them, and there were twenty of us standing between them and our old people, our children, and our women.

The one who stood in front of the others made a noise. It may have been words, but it was no language we had heard before. It was hard to believe a human being could make such sounds. Those sounds made some of our people wonder if these strange men were from the world of spirits. As soon as the one in front stopped growling, though, Casts Light stepped forward.

Casts Light was a brave man. His dreams in the past had showed him how to do good things and he had a reputation as a healer. He advanced on the Ice-Hearts, holding an Eagle feather in front of him as if it were a burning branch. He shook it at the One In Front and was about to say something, but his words never left his mouth. There was a sudden flash as the One In Front's blade swept through the air. The Eagle feather fell to the ground in two pieces and Casts Light fell beside it, his head almost cut from his body. It was an evil deed and we waited no longer. Whether men or spirits, we had to drive them out. The One In Front was grabbing now at the pieces of meat drying above the fire. We let fly with our weapons.

Most of our arrows and spears bounced off their hard bodies, but the Ice-Hearts began making a great noise and moved back towards the door. Their strange eyes flashed in the firelight and they swung their weapons at us, but we stayed back, picking up our arrows as they bounced off and firing again. Now the women were shouting out war songs. "Do not let these People of Ice kill our children," they cried, and it urged us on. Then an arrow hurt the One In Front. Whether by luck or good aim, it went into one of the few places which was not armored on his body — it struck him in the eye. His hands went up to his face and he fell backwards. The others grabbed him and dragged him with them. They were out the door now, going back along the tracks Grandmother Moon showed us they had made in the deep soft snow as they came upon our longhouse. Another of the Ice-Hearts fell, a spear piercing his neck. He, too, was carried off by the others. They moved quickly, those big men. Most of us were not quick to follow.

That was when I called my three friends aside. They had come with me once when we went to raid against the People Who Live Where The Dawn Begins. I held up my snowshoes and made a half circle motion over the hill. They understood. If we went that way we might be able to cut off some of the Ice-Hearts from the others. And so it happened.

When we came back to the longhouse everyone, the living and the dead, was there. There was a smell in the air like that of a slaughtered deer and there was dark blood frozen in the snow at the door. Sounds of mourning filled the air. But as we pushed the two big men ahead of us, the sounds turned into shouts of wonder. We were carrying the weapons of the Ice-Hearts, and they had been so well armed that each of us had something. I carried a big shield which was cold to the touch as stone. Eats Like A Bear had one of the long knives and so did Eagle Circling. Sore Eyes had chosen an axe, the best choice of all of us. He would use that axe for many years clearing space for cornfields and cutting poles for lodges. Big Duck, who had defeated them, carried two smaller knives which he juggled from hand to hand. He was trying to look serious and strong, but the laughter kept creeping back into his eyes.

The women came close. Some of them made remarks about the size of the men and jabbed sticks at them. They were making jokes, but they were angry. Two women no longer had husbands and there were children without a father now. If we had handed the Ice-Hearts over to the women then, they would have killed them. Instead, we took our captives to the fire in the center. There we removed the armor from them. Without their heavy coats the men were still big, but they were thin. Their ribs showed and the bones of their shoulders stuck out like the knobs of war clubs. That was why they attacked us then? For food because they were starving?

"But there is plenty of game around here," said Pretty Eyes, the wife of Eagle Circling.

"Maybe they only know how to fight and not how to hunt," I suggested. Some of the people looked at me as if they thought I was crazy, but later on they would see I was right. The weapons the Ice-Hearts carried were not for hunting game animals. The place they came from must have been strange indeed if it bred men who knew only how to kill other human beings and not how to hunt to keep themselves and their families alive.

We tied the hands of the two big men and made them sit down near the fire. Near them were the bodies of the two their people killed. Outside, the Sun, our Elder Brother, was rising. He must have been disappointed, for he is the one who loves fighting and war the best and it all had happened while our Grandmother, the moon, was in the sky. To us, though, it was neither day nor night now. Something had happened which never had happened before. It was the time to talk and listen to wise voices.

Each person who wished to speak was given a chance. Many wished to kill the men right away.

"We have been calling these creatures Ice-Hearts," said a man named Wood Tick, "because they are like the monsters in the old stories. Let us see if their hearts really are made of ice. If we cut them out, then we can tell."

"Let us see how brave they are," said a woman named Swaying Reeds. "Let us see if they know any Death Songs."

I, too, had my chance to speak. "These people," I said, "they belong to me and my friends, I think. We caught them. We give them, though, to everyone here. All of you can decide what to do with them. I am not very wise and I cannot say what should be done. If we keep them, though, they may be good workers. Many people here have relatives who were adopted in the past. Now they are part of us. Two of our people are dead. Now we have two captives. Maybe someone will take them in. Maybe they can learn to talk like real human beings and tell us about the place they came from. I have said enough. That is all I have to say."

So we continued to talk. The time came to eat and we untied the hands of the two men. They were surprised, but they ate with us, ate like men who are hungry but also grateful to be fed. Then we talked further. The Sun was going down when everyone had spoken. I had been pleased to hear words like my own, though spoken better and clearer — for the waters of age run deeper and hold more fish than the swift streams of youth. The Old Men Who Wear The Horns of Office, those who spoke for us at the meetings of the Great League, they had seen things as I saw them. That was good. They had been listening, as they always do, to the Clan Mothers, those women whose words are sometimes not heard in council, but who point the way to any decision.

In the end, the two men were adopted. We made this clear to them by signs which they understood.

The younger-looking one, whose face was very thin with a big beak of a nose under a thatch of hair the color of fire was adopted by the widow of old Goes In The Corner.

"He will be my son," she said. "I'm going to call him Woodpecker."

The other was adopted by the family of Casts Light. There were grim scars on his chest and thighs which showed he had been a warrior for some time. The hair on his head was the color of autumn grass, but he was hairy all over his body and especially on his chest and those hairs were very black. Bear Chest is what we called him. That was appropriate in more ways than we knew. The Bear Clan adopted him and the Bear Clan has always been known for its healers. It turned out that Bear Chest knew how to set broken limbs and knew other ways of healing which helped many. Casts Light's uncle taught him other things about medicine and the fame of Bear Chest as a doctor spread among our people as years passed.

They never left us. They grew fat from our food and married good women who gave us many children. At first they called us "Sgah-lay-leens," a word from their old language. But as they learned our words, the past and their old way of talking fell away from them as leaves fall from the maples during the Moon of Falling Leaves and with spring the green buds of real human speech opened from their mouths.

We saw no more of their people. Stories came to us over the years. The People of the Dawn passed on tales of big men like our Ice-Hearts. They came in canoes larger than a lodge and fought the way our Ice-Hearts fought. But all of them were wiped out and no more boats came. They were like the storms which blow in sometimes from the big salt water. Those storms are strong at first, but they falter and die after moving inland. Storms come and go, but the Earth stays.

I, Fox Looking Around, am a very old man. Woodpecker and Bear Chest have been dead for many seasons and some of you are their children. Your skins are pale, perhaps, and some of you have eyes the color of the sky. But you are real human beings, just as your fathers became real human beings after we adopted them. Your children will look more like us still. That is the way it has always been. But I do not think, as do all the rest of our people, that the story of the Ice-Hearts is over. True, we learned that the Ice-Hearts are men. We learned that laughter is a great weapon, a defense which can melt a cold heart. But I believe that one day more of those people of the storm, those people who know how to kill other human beings but do not know how to grow crops or hunt, will come to this place where we live. There may be more of them then and they may have strange ideas of keeping the land for themselves the way you might keep a favorite ball or a pair of moccasins.

Listen, for this is the way Woodpecker explained it to me after he had lived with us for many seasons.

"Fox," he said, "You are my brother and I never had a brother before. You are closer to me now than Eric . . . Bear Chest, for he is a man with a good heart but he does not think very much. So I want to tell you something, something you must promise to pass on to our children. I tell you this for you understand better than the others who just nod and then look away when I tell them. We came to this place to take land. We came from a place where there was not land enough for our people. Instead, this land took us. It has not ended, though. Others like my people will come someday. But I have thought and thought hard and this is what I think. I think that more people will die next time. You will have to fight and keep on fighting for a long time. But this land of yours is strong, Fox Looking Around. It is strong and you know that. If you stay close to this land, if you do not give it up, it will win again. Tell that to our children."

And, all of my life, that is what I have done. This is where my story ends.

Peter Schuyler and the Mohican; A Story of Old Albany

When Peter Schuyler was the Mayor of Albany, he used to walk along the busy docks on the wide Hudson River where ships sailed in and out each day. One day, on his customary walk, he saw a Mohican man sitting with his feet dangling over the edge of one of the piers, watching the ships and the river and quite obviously doing nothing useful. Mayor Schuyler was a man much devoted to doing useful work. So he approached the Indian and said, "You there, why don't you do some work, you lazy good-for-nothing?"

"Why don't you work, Mayor?" said the Mohican.

"What?" said Schuyler. "I work all the time. I just do it within my head."

"Ah-huh," said the Mohican, "I begin to understand. You just give me some work to do and then I will do it."

"Good!" said Schuyler, "You can go to my barn and kill the calf there for me. We have been intending to eat that calf and there is a man who wants the skin."

"I agree," said the Indian. "First, though, you must pay me. It is a long walk to your barn."

Though Schuyler thought all Indians were lazy, he knew that they could be trusted to keep their word. So he handed over a shilling in advance and the Indian left. In a bit more than a hour, he came back to the place where Schuyler still stood, watching the ships.

"Well," said Schuyler, "where is the skin?"

"You only asked me to kill the calf," said the Mohican. "If you wanted me to skin it, you should have asked me. Give me another shilling and I will skin it and dress it out for you."

Reluctantly, the Mayor pulled out another coin and the Mohican set out for the farm. An hour later he came back with the skin and handed it to the Mayor. But as he gave it to him, he said. "Those dogs there at your farm look as if they want to eat that calf."

"What?" said Schuyler. "Did you not hang it up where they couldn't reach it?"

"Hang it up?" said the Indian. "You only asked me to skin it and dress it out. Give me another shilling and I will run back and hang it. But you must do so quickly. Those dogs looked hungry."

By now, Mayor Schuyler was getting angry. He reached into his pocket and found he had only a two-shilling piece. "Here," he said, shoving the coin at the Indian, "give me back a shilling in change."

The Mohican man did so and then trotted off, Schuyler's coins jingling in his pouch. While he was gone, Mayor Schuyler thought over all that had just happened. There was no way he would let an Indian get the better of him. The Mayor decided he would teach this Mohican a lesson he would not forget. Taking out a piece of paper, he wrote on it, *The bearer of this is a rogue. Give him a good beating.* Then he signed it, folded it and sealed it.

When the Mohican returned an hour later, Schuyler smiled. "Would you like to earn another shilling, my friend?" he said.

"Certainly, my friend," said the Indian, holding out his hand for the coin.

"Good," said the Mayor, "This note must be delivered to the Captain up at the fort. I want you to see that it is delivered into his hands. He will give you something special for doing this. Then I want you to come back to this same spot and when you see me again you can tell me what you think about things."

The Mohican took the note and started on his way. However, though he could not read, he did not go far before he began to think about things, indeed. The smile on the Mayor's face as he left him had been much too broad. As the Mohican walked along, he saw coming his way one of Schuyler's English servants, a young man with a reputation for disliking Indians. The Mohican walked up to him and held the paper so that the young Englishman could see the Mayor's seal on it.

"Do you see this?" the Mohican said. "The Mayor wants this note delivered to the Captain at the fort. The person who delivers this note will be given something special, but I am not certain how to take it to the Captain."

"Why are all you Indians so stupid?" said the young Englishman, grabbing the sealed note out of the Mohican's hand. "I shall see that it gets to the Captain." Then the young Englishman headed for the fort, eager to get what was coming to him.

The Mohican man followed at a prudent distance. When he saw

the Captain read the note and then ordered his men to take hold of the young Englishman and beat him, the Mohican turned around and went back to the wharf.

Later that same day, when Mayor Schuyler came looking for him, he found the Mohican back in his familiar spot, watching the ships go by and dangling his feet in the water.

"You ignorant savage," said the Mayor, "I thought I told you to take that paper to the Captain."

"You said the note was to be delivered into his hands. I saw that it was delivered. Then, having done so, I came back here as you asked."

"Hmph," said the Mayor. Perhaps you think you made four shillings, but you did not. That second shilling I gave you was made of lead. It is worthless."

"I know," said the Mohican man, "that is why I gave it back to you in change for the two-shilling piece."

"You rascal," said Mayor Schuyler, "How is it that you manage to get by with such impertinence?"

"Ahh," said the Mohican, smiling as he watched the ships on the river, "I do it within my head."

Going Home

"Look, Tommy, down there in the valley. Look at all those little houses the white people have made. Look at how they are all like little boxes, those houses in that little town of theirs. They always like to build in the valleys like those, the white people."

The new Ford van rolled along the Thruway as Jake Marsh pointed with one long brown finger out the window on the passenger side, the imitation "Indin" accent coming out from between lips held carefully unmoving. The half-smile of trickster was on his face, a can of ginger ale in his other hand. Behind the wheel, Tom Hill shook his head and laughed silently.

"Yes," Tom said, "yes."

"Oooh, Tommy, maybe there is a college in that town. Yes, there is a college there. Maybe it is the college where Sonny is going to school. He has been in college a long time."

"Twelve years," Tom said, coughing.

"He is always writing us for money, Tommy. He is a good boy. He is doing well in the college. Some day we are going to go and see him. If he ever tells us where the college is. All of us are going to go see him."

"All of us," Tom said, "all hundred and twenty of us."

"Yes, we will go there for his graduation and have a give-away. We will give away many blankets. Then he can come home. They say at the Agency they have a good job for him. Janitor. That will be a good job for an Indin boy. It will have vacation time."

"Retirement benefits," Tom said, trying to keep his face straight.

"Tommy, you know he has a girl there at the college. But he will not tell us about her. I think mebbe she is white."

"She's white."

"But Sonny won't have any children by her. He is going to come back home and marry Dolores Antelope. She comes from a good family, even if they are a little stupid. Yes, when he comes home he will marry Dolores. She has been waiting for him."

"Only twenty years now," Tom said. Then he started laughing.

Jake Marsh laughed too. They laughed at the person Jake had been for a while, that gentle, bemused tone in the voice, that simple way of saying and seeing which — even as they laughed at it — was laughing at them, laughing with them. Jake drained the can of ginger ale and began striking his palm against the dashboard, beating out the rhythm of a 49-er:

"Someday we will be together
till eternity, ah whey ya hi ya hi..."

He sang it in a low voice first, then higher with each repetition. Tom strained his own vocal cords to stay with it until both of them were singing in voices thin as the last note of a coyote's call. Tom's throat felt tight and good. The song stopped and they listened for a while to the silence. Then Jake began striking the dashboard again, trying to find another beat.

"Funny," he said, "when I used to drink I could remember a thousand songs. Now it's hard to remember one." He crushed the ginger ale can and put it into the plastic litter bag hanging from the knob of the glove compartment.

The hills tolled up from the river near the road. On top of a few hills single pine trees stood. They looked like men with arms held out from their sides, waiting for something. Tom thought that for a moment, then shook his head. No, not men, trees. The trees looked like trees. It had been a long time since he had seen them this way.

"When I was at Fort Grant," he said. Then he stopped. He had to let the words come together in the right way. Jake sat, waiting for him. Five miles passed. A red-tail hawk glided over the road, heading west. Tom took in a deep breath. "There weren't too many Indians there. Most of them were Pimas or Papagoes, in for stealing something while they were drunk, most of them. One or two for murder — the murderers are the ones you can trust, you know. It's the ones who forge checks that are the worst. You can't trust them. But the murderers, you could always trust them. One was a guy from Oklahoma. His name was Harold Buffalo. His uncle is that painter. I met his sister in Tulsa once."

"Was her name Mary?" Jake said.

"Yes, it was. She had a little boy, too."

"She's on the East Coast now. Working for *Akwesasne Notes.*"

"Ah-hah," Tom said. He shifted his hands on the wheel and pointed with his lips at the sign which read REST AREA. Jake shook his head and they passed the turn-off without slowing down. Tom took another deep breath. "There wasn't anything in the prison for us then. It was so far out in the desert it cost wives and girlfriends more than twenty dollars to come and visit. It was called a 'Rehabilitation Center.' For rehabilitation, ree-hah-bill-ih-tay-shun, they would have us build walls. Long stone walls. They looked like the Great Wall of China, except they were about four feet tall, the walls we built. They had us build them at the base of the mountain that rose behind the prison. That mountain was beautiful. You could feel its breath. But there was nothing for us in Fort Grant. So we asked to be allowed to have a sweat lodge. It would have to be sponsored by someone, we were told. There were sweat lodges in other prisons, but none there — even though now there were twenty of us who were Indians and we knew we needed it. Damn."

"Right rear tire," Jake said.

Tom pulled the van over to the side of the road. The flat tire went wha-that wha-that on the pavement and then growled into the gravel. Both men got out and stretched. They walked up the grassy bank and sat down. It was a crisp day in early September. The air was sweet as spring water. Jake leaned on one elbow to look closely at a small plant.

"It says I should pick it."

"Your uncle was the medicine man," Tom said. He looked at the plant. They were both smiling, but Jake pulled the small plant up and wrapped it in his handkerchief, leaving a little tobacco on the ground near the grains of gravel which came up with the roots. They walked back to the van and began to change the tire. They worked with the quick ease of men who had spent many years doing that sort of thing. When they were done they spat, wiped their hands on the seats of their jeans and got back in.

Jake sat behind the wheel. He started the engine. "What did you do next?" he said. He put the truck into gear.

"We did it their way first. We went to the prison chaplain. There was only one. For all faiths — Methodist, Baptist, Catholic, Mormon, Jewish, even the Black Muslims. He was a Catholic priest from Boston, Father Milley. He was so thin we use to say he didn't dare cross his legs for fear he'd cut his knees. He told us that a sweat lodge was not possible. That was when Harold Buffalo spoke up. 'There is going to be a sweat lodge here, Sir,' he said. 'When something like that is going to happen, you can't stop it.'"

"Did they interpret that as a threat?"

"They interpreted that as a threat. First they thought of transferring Harold. Then they remembered all the times he had asked to be transferred from Fort Grant and decided that wasn't much of a punishment, maybe even it was what he wanted them to do. Finally they decided to cut off his privileges. When they let him out of the hole, he was told he could no longer have rec with the other men. But he didn't mind. He started to run by himself every day. First he ran a mile. Then he ran two miles. By the time they decided to let him back into population he was running ten miles every day. He had been a Green Beret and he knew a lot about survival in the desert. That worried the prison authorities because everyone in Arizona remembered The Fox."

"I heard of him in Nevada." Jake said. "Another Green Beret."

"The Fox escaped from Florence. He'd been in for killing four men — two of them police. He knew he'd never be allowed to get away, so he didn't even try to get to Mexico. He didn't try to escape any further. He just stayed out in the desert near the prison. Nights he would sneak into the camps of the men hunting him and steal their food. He even climbed back over the walls of the prison and left his calling card — right where the Captain stepped in it first thing next morning. It took them a long time to catch The Fox, but they say they finally did. Caught him in a box canyon and shot him to pieces. But none of the other inmates ever saw his body. Some say he is still out there or he finally did make it to Mexico. So the authorities kept a close eye on Harold because they remembered The Fox. But all Harold did was run, just run further and faster each day, around and around inside the prison fence."

Tom pulled out a pack of Camels and shook two loose. Jake took one and lit both cigarettes with his lighter. The lighter was covered with red and blue beads making the pattern of a thunderbird. The smoke was blue inside the cab of the blue van. The smell of the tobacco was strong. Jake nodded to the right and Tom nodded. They took the exit. There was a police car pulled over near the toll booth. Tom opened the glove compartment and slid the automatic pistol out without looking at it, his eyes straight ahead. He put the gun between his legs and covered it with his kerchief. They stopped at the toll booth.

Jake smiled at the fortyish woman with dark hair who leaned out of the booth. She looked as if her feet hurt, but she smiled back.

"Indins get to use this road free, don't they?" Jake said.

"You tell that to the people at the other end when you got on?" she said. She showed her teeth in a wide smile. "That's a nice ring you got there. Make it yourself?"

"They didn't give me any ticket when we got on. And I did make the ring. You like it?"

"I like that turquoise. Blue is a good color." She waved them on. "Have a nice day."

They turned onto the four-lane which would take them into the city.

"I think," Tom said, "the state cop in the cruiser wasn't really asleep. I think he was watching which way we were going."

"They aren't all stupid these days," Jake said. "He saw us taking 81 south, right?"

"Right. No one following us now, though."

Jake looked in the rearview mirror, then quickly swung the van to the left, crossing the divider in the center of the road and heading back towards the north. He took the exit which led to the road around the city.

"Unless they got a chopper up top, we're okay for now."

"What happened next," Tom said, "is that one morning Harold Buffalo was just gone. They found his pillows rolled up under his blankets and even the dogs couldn't pick up his scent. They looked everywhere and couldn't find a trace. He was gone that day and all that night. But next morning we looked up towards the top of the mountain above the prison just at dawn and we saw the light of the fire and the smoke rising. It took them the better part of the day to work their way up there. They found him still sitting in front of the fire where he had been sitting to pray and greet the dawn. 'It is a good day,' he said. Then he said, 'We are going to have a sweat lodge in Fort Grant.' Everybody had seen his fire and knew what was happening, so they hardly even beat him up before they brought him back down. By now the reporters from Tucson had come to the prison to get the story and they'd seen the fire, too. When they took him in to the warden, Harold told the man he knew how to get out without anyone seeing him. He could do it whenever he wanted. He could teach other people how to do it. In fact, there were at least nineteen other men right now who knew how to do it. He told him that. Then he said, 'Sir, we want to have a sweat lodge.' Three days later, we had our first sweat."

They had bypassed the city now and they left the four-lane for a smaller road, then turned onto one of dirt which wound through the hills. The vegetation was thick and close to the road's edge. A rabbit crossed in front of them, then a raccoon. Jake slowed the blue van. They were passing a roadside dump where car bodies and garbage were strewn.

"Indian recycling station," Tom said. He took the crushed ginger ale can out of the litter bag and tossed it. It spun through the air and bounced off the cracked side of an old GE refrigerator.

"If I was a state cop," Jake said, "I would set up a little roadblock at the edge of the reservation. Maybe around the next corner where this runs back into the state road." He slowed the van down to a stop and set the emergency brake.

Tom took the duffel bag out of the back. He slung it over his shoulder. "Well," he said, patting the side of the van, "they won't have to walk far to find this. So long, Big Blue."

"They're going to catch us," Jake said. He had picked up a long stick from the roadside and was whittling carefully at it with the long knife he'd taken from the sheath at his side. The turquoise ring glinted as his hand moved with small, sure strokes.

"Not before we get to the mountain top," Tom said. It was impossible to see his eyes behind the dark glasses, but Jake knew they were hard and black and laughing.

"Yes," Jake said. "It is good to go home." They moved together into the trees.

Jed's Grandfather

Jed slowly worked the handle of the backyard pitcher pump. He watched the water lap from side to side in waves as he tilted the bucket back and forth. The patterns of the dream were still going through his head. They hadn't been washed away with the first splash of water from the trough, water so cold that a paper-thin layer of ice still had to be brushed away these early spring mornings. Washing his face usually cleared whatever cobwebs of sleep still clung to his face and his thoughts, but it hadn't happened this morning. The dream was still with him.

The swallows had flown up now. The red sun was a finger's width above the hill. He looked up and watched the swallows darting, stitching the face of the sky the way his mother's needle covered a piece of cloth. The other birds, shorter-winged, fluttered in groups, as if afraid to fly by themselves the way the swallows did. The swallows were the adventurous ones. He remembered how his grandfather first pointed out to him the way a swallow can dart down to the surface of a lake and scoop up a mouthful of water without landing. They had watched swallows doing that, drinking from the pond below the house that day last blueberry season when Grandfather rowed him out to The Island.

Usually the sight of the swallows in the morning sky would drive everything else out of his thoughts. He'd arch his back, lift his chin, hold out his arms, hearing his Grandfather's soft voice guiding him. "You want to be a swallow, Jeddy? You can do it. Just feel the wind under ye. That's it."

That wouldn't work this morning. The dream was too strong. He was in the boat, dark water widening between them. The old man stood there on The Island, unaware of the great dark wave coming at him from behind. His eyes were on Jed, but Jed couldn't call out. He couldn't move his arms. He wanted to turn into a swallow, fly out and rescue him, but he was paralyzed. Then the water between them began to open like a crack in the earth. . .

"Jed!" It was his mother's voice. Jed looked up. The bucket was filled and overflowing around his feet. A chicken was scurrying around the edge of the spreading water, now and then lifting a foot and shaking it as the water touched it. Jed carried the bucket into the kitchen.

His parents were at the table. Jed bent his arms and arched his back, hefting the bucket up onto the sink shelf.

"You're getting stronger ever day, son," his father said, thin hand around a steaming mug. Behind him the wood stove crackled, a sound Jed had always loved. The steam from his father's coffee rose through the cold morning air of the kitchen. Jed could smell the coffee. It was a good smell, just as good but not quite the same as that smell when he ground the beans in the coffee mill with its blue enamel sides. But even the good smell of the coffee couldn't drive away the dream. It was there, between him and the things which were good and pleasant in his life, there the way a thick fog comes between a boat and the land. He was on the boat. He didn't know which way was home.

Jed's mother smiled at him, wiped her hands on her apron. It was the first time he had really noticed the way his mother always wiped her hands on her apron before she spoke when they were at the table. She used the same care with her words that she did in making their food. All around Jed were familiar things, things known and loved, but he was seeing them for the first time . . . the small crystal dog in the east window where a bull's-eye pane of glass split the sun like a prism and painted a rainbow on the wall near the stairs . . . the woodbox with its splintery top which sometimes snagged his left thumb when he went for an armful of kindling . . . the rocking chair which always caught the last rays of the setting sun, the chair which was empty now. . .

"He just takes after his . . ." his mother was saying. She stopped in mid-sentence. Jed finished the sentence in his own mind. *He takes after his grandfather.* Jed's father was a good man, hard-working, but he never had the strength of his wife's people, the Sabaels. That was why he worked as a clerk at the store in town three miles from the farm. It was Jed's grandfather, straight as an ash, who always did the work around the farm. Jed was only ten, but he was already as strong as his father.

"Jed," his mother said, her hands smoothing her apron, "you aren't eating."

The pancakes were dry in his mouth. He knew they were good. They were the pancakes his mother was famous for at church socials. They were light and smelled of the goodness of a summer wheatfield, but he couldn't taste them. Instead he tasted the moist air within the fog, felt the pressure of the building storm throb around his temples as the great dark wave lifted.

Jed's father was saying something to his mother. What was it? Starving himself? Jed hadn't heard the words for sure over the roaring of the wave.

"Are you sure?" his mother said.

"You're his daughter," Jed's father answered. He spoke in the same quiet voice Jed heard him use when he answered a customer who asked what to buy to get rid of potato bugs or whether the percale was what she really wanted for her money's worth.

Jed's mother rose and walked over to the stove. She took the plate which had been warming there and covered it with a cloth. She put the cloth-covered plate, some silverware and a stoppered bottle into a basket. Jed recognized the basket. It was one Grandfather made. He remembered the sounds of the mallet as his grandfather pounded the side of the felled ash tree to break loose the withes he'd trim to size. His grandfather had shown him the steps many times, shown him by doing. He felt as if the way of making a basket was woven into him the way the pattern of a web is woven into a spider's limbs. It was a craft passed down for more generations that the Sabaels could count, passed down before Jed's father's people had stepped from their ships onto these shores. For a moment the thought of Grandfather's sure hands weaving a basket drove away the dream. Then the pounding of the mallet became the pounding of whitecaps against the side of the boat and he saw the old man's figure made small by the lifting darkness.

"Take this down to the Little House, Jed," his mother said. She was holding the basket out to him. Jed looked up into her eyes for a moment and then reached out his hand.

No smoke was rising from the chimney. Had it been rising it would have traced a perfect line up the face of the mountains and sky above Indian Lake. That was the way smoke rose on spring mornings such as this from the small one-roomed house his grandfather had built where the field fell away, green becoming the grey of stone, then the blue of water. A small boat was tied to a pole that jutted out of the water. The boat moved with the water the way a horse moves when tied to a rail. . . not pulling hard enough to break free, hardly even putting a strain on its tether, but showing in its motion how anxious it is to be on its way. The boat was still there. But there was no smoke.

Jed drew in a breath, feeling it catch in his stiff throat. But before he could speak he heard his grandfather's voice.

"Come," the old man called out, making that simple word one of many meanings. It meant he knew who was there. It meant Jed was welcome. It meant something else, too. It was like the words in the old language his grandfather seldom spoke, the language few people knew he knew. Jed pulled gently at the locust post which held up the small open gate. It creaked as he pulled at it, but the old wood was still firm. A locust post can stay in the ground a hundred years and still bend any nail you're fool enough to try to drive into it. A hundred years.

Jed went in. Joseph Sabael was sitting on the edge of his cot. There was a blanket around his shoulders and he was wearing his woolens, but his feet were bare. There was no rug on the floor, no fire in the stove. It was cold in the Little House, but not as cold as Jed had thought it would be. There was a faint odor in the air, one Jed had not really noticed before. It confused him.

"That's just how the cancer smells, Jeddy," his grandfather said. "Don't pay it no mind. It's just as natural as anything else."

Jed looked at him. John Sabael had always been a tall man, but never one whose frame put on bulk. His shoulders had been broad, but not heavy. His arms had always been long and sinewy like the others in the town who worked the land or the big woods, not the ham-thick sort of arm which turned to softness with age. Like an ash tree's limbs, that was how his grandfather's arms had seemed. But now there was a different look to the old man. His eyes had fallen back into their sockets and one could see the bones beneath the skin in his arms. As he sat, hands clasping the blanket about him, it seemed as if his shoulders were folding in around his chest. Jed held out the basket.

"Mama sent you this," he said.

"I be glad she let you come," Grandfather said. He didn't reach out his hands for the basket.

"I wasn't sure I wanted to until now," Jed said. He heard his own voice as if it were the voice of a stranger.

His grandfather nodded. Very slowly, he got up from the bed. It seemed to Jed as if he were watching something happen as strange and wonderful, as magical as a tree uprooting itself and stepping across the woodlot. Joseph Sabael walked very slowly to the back door of the Little House. Jed opened it for him. Together they stepped out into the light from the open water, a light which made Jed's eyes squint against the brightness of it all. His grandfather sat down carefully in the rough wooden chair which faced The Island. Again Jed smelled that strange odor, but now he knew what it was and he was not confused. It was his grandfather's death.

Gulls began swooping down in front of them. They were grey and white. From their yellow beaks came those raucous squawks which seemed to Jed to be the one thing which linked them to the rock they flew up from. Those voices, rough and filled with the earth, were all that kept the gulls from flying up and up forever until they blended with the sky.

His grandfather made a small motion with his hand and Jed opened the basket. He removed the cloth from the plate. The heat rose up to touch the back of his hand. With his fingers he broke the pancakes up into small pieces. Then, piece by piece, he tossed them up into the air. Swooping, diving, squabbling in mid-air, the gulls caught them all. Not one piece touched the waveless lake.

The Fox Den

It is a Sunday afternoon in mid-spring. The air is hot and still, the day unseasonably dry. The rains which usually fill the streams of the Adirondack foothill slopes have not come. In the small valley formed by the flow of the creek, the water is quick over tumbled stones, yet shallower than in the years of the recent past. The steep slope to the west of the stream is topped by a great white pine tree, one which has stood for more centuries than the stream below its arching branches has known the name given it by white settlers: Bell Brook.

Two of the tree's roots arch out from the bank, almost like the buttresses of a cathedral. Between those roots two men stand, shovels in their hands. Neither of the men know that the hill on which they stand was formed more than ten thousand years ago at the end of the last Ice Age. Then, as the flow of the waters from the great mountains of cold slowed, scoured soil was deposited here as a terminal moraine.

The men have been digging into the fox den which opens, hidden from a casual eye, between those two roots. On the bank above them a collie dog sits, her tongue lolling out. She is lazily watchful, her paws around a large rock which now blocks the other entrance to the den. It is a piece of sedimentary rock. It holds within it deep memory of the time when all the land around was ocean. The shapes of sea shells and a perfectly shaped trilobite stand out on the surface, made darker and clearer by the saliva which drips from the collie's mouth.

The two men have been digging for half an hour and now they are resting. Sand sticks to their necks and their faces are blackened from the backs of their hands where they reached up to wipe away the sweat. My grandfather's dark black hair glistens with moisture. His eyes are quiet and bright as ebony. The dirt shows less on his dark skin than on the face of Harry Dunham, his brother-in-law. But Harry's face is brown also, burned tan by years of farming and working with the horses he loves and is always trading. They each take a deep breath, tap their shovels against a root to knock off moist sand, and begin to dig again.

Suddenly the vixen bolts from the den, right between my Grandfather's legs.

"Jess, there she goes!" Harry shouts. My Grandfather does not move. Instead, he whistles.

The collie leaps to her feet in a half circle and runs after the fox. Her belly is so low to the ground that she plows through the leaves. Her feet leave deep marks in the leaf mold and earth. Thousands of tiny roots which hold the soil the way fine thread holds the pattern on a piece of embroidery are exposed. The fox snaps and dodges. The snarls of the dog and the high voice of the fox blend. Then it is over. The dog stands shaking a limp body. The dog tosses the fox once, then again and backs off. The fox lies there on its side, mouth wide, eyes open yet without sight. Its black muzzle is flecked with blood.

My Grandfather reaches into the den. "She's killed 'em all," he says.

Trapped, hearing the scrape of the shovels, ranging back and forth between the blocked hole and the smells and sounds of men, digging frantically at the rock which blocked escape (paws worn raw from the rough stone), she went crazy and killed her litter.

My Grandfather reaches in and brings out the small warm bodies of the little foxes. Then he shoves head and shoulders into the hole.

"This un's not dead."

He pulls out a tiny cub. Its throat is torn, but it whines feebly as he stands up with it in his hands.

"Might as well kill it now. It'll jus grow up t' kill yer chickens again." Harry hefts the shovel.

"I'm takin' it home to Marion."

Marion Flora Dunham was my Grandmother's name before she married my Grandfather. Flora Marion Bowman was my mother's name and her two first names were those of her grandmother. So it went back for generations: a Flora Marion birthing a Marion Flora whose daughter would again bear a grandmother's name. Other women might lose their names in marriage, but it was not completely so for the women of my grandmother's line, women who made the family decisions more than the men did, women who married men who — though strong and sure of themselves — had a quality of gentleness and quiet about them, a way of listening to their women as if hearing an ancient matriarchal voice from a past most other men forgot. So, when she married my grandfather, a man of little education and dubious ancestry, some were surprised, but to me, looking back at it over the decades, hearing my grandfather's soft voice, it seems it was as it should have been. There was more to it than just a wealthy landowner's daughter marrying a half-breed hired man.

My Grandmother sent her husband and her brother to dig out the fox den. The chickens were disappearing. That very morning the prized rooster, a Rhode Island Red, was taken. She'd seen the fox's brush disappearing into the sumacs at the edge of the field across Middle Grove Road just after hearing the squawks of the hens. Jess and Harry knew where the den was. Foxes had denned at the base of that pine for as long as Dunhams — or Bowmans (whether by that anglicized name or the older Abenaki of Abowmsawin) — had been in that country. My Grandfather went the half mile up the creek, found red feathers and a recently gnawed bone on the mound of brown earth. He came back to get Harry and two shovels.

My Grandfather walked into the kitchen with the fox in his hands.

"Flora," my Grandmother said, "run get my sewing basket and the biggest needle."

Then, the blood of the fox staining her apron patterned with tiny blue and purple flowers (blue and purple as the violets the men's feet brushed through as they walked the bank of the crick), she sewed its torn throat.

My Grandmother often talked about that fox.

"It played with a ball of yarn just like a kitten. Why, even the collie got to accept it. It'd run around her like a puppy, biting her nose and nipping at her tail while she'd pretend it wasn't really a fox at all."

They kept the fox in the house. It had house trained as easily as a cat, waiting to go outside then digging a little hole in the earth and scraping dirt back over it when it was done. Some people came to see it, but a tamed fox was not such a big thing for many people in Greenfield in those days. That was the way it was then. People would, especially those who lived back more in the hills and on the more remote farmsteads, have wild animals for pets — most often raccoons or a crow taken as a fledgling from its nest. Wild animals could live for a time among humans. The boundaries were not as clear then as now.

The magic of an age when everything in the natural world was known to have a voice and when some women and men could hear those voices — if not speak and understand them — was still present. It circled at nights around the farms where there were no streetlamps to keep away the dark and the sounds of cicadas and peepers and the call of the whip-poor-will and the nighthawk were louder than the roar of machines.

The boundaries were still there, though. One day Reddy crossed over one of those boundaries and there was no going back. He was shot as he was chasing chickens at the Middlebrooks place a mile down the road. When Truman saw the collar on him he brought him back to my grandparents and my mother. My Grandfather buried him on the pine hill above Bell Brook. He did not mention to my Grandmother that a new burrow had been opened near the one they dug out. Instead, he strengthened the chicken wire around the hen house. No fox ever got in to take one of their chickens again, though twice weasels came and my Grandfather had to shoot them by the light of the lantern as they stood, staring, mouths still red from the throats of a dozen hens, their bodies small and snake-sinewy and brown.

Two years ago, on my 40th birthday, I walked the old fields. When I came to the edge of the woods which follow both sides of the stream bank like long arms I stopped. It seemed there was motion in the sumacs and honey locusts which are reclaiming the northeast edge of the field, colonists for an invasion of trees. A bird flew up suddenly, wings flapping open like a Japanese fan, and then a small orange dog followed it out into the field. A fox, I realized. Our eyes met and it stopped. It was less than twenty feet away but it did not run. Instead, it sat down. Then it yawned as both dogs and foxes yawn, opening its mouth wide and turning its head slightly as it did so. Its eyes turned back to mine and I began to sing. Its eyes half-closed as I sang the song which a Pueblo Indian friend taught me. I stopped singing and it got up from its haunches, moved a few steps closer, then sat again. It looked up at me as if to say, "Well, isn't there more to that song?" I sang again, the sun of that autumn day on both of our faces. Finally, I walked away, leaving it still sitting there in the meadow. I took that meeting as a kind of affirmation.

There was no collar around the neck of my fox, yet it was, for that one moment and forever after, as close to me as the one my mother and grandparents kept as a pet was to them two decades before I was born. And when I walked this spring up along Bell Brook to the old white pine, I saw fresh earth loosened around its roots.

Code Talker

Thomas J. Fox is what it says on the chart at the foot of my bed. Thomas J. Fox. I guess that is my name. At least it is one of the names I answer to. There's other information there about me, too, all of which is more or less accurate. Weight: 180 pounds. Height: 5'7". Religious denomination: Methodist. (But don't ask me how they found that out!) Age: 74, give or take a decade. It doesn't list my occupation but if it did I suppose it would say something like "Professional Indian-in-residence, currently recuperating from wounds received in the line of duty at the Quadrangle Mall." It ain't easy.

As I lean my head back against my pillow waiting for Peter's visit I can see out the window. It is eleven in the morning and the birds are quiet as the sun gets hotter. Early in the morning I can hear the call of a cardinal from outside that window, even when they have it shut. I can hear the purple finches quarrelling with each other in the upper branches of the blue spruce out there on the hospital lawn and the pigeons cooing and complaining from the ledges over the window. If I sit up I can see down to the street outside and the empty space across the street where there used to be a building. A building I knew pretty darn well. The old Paramount Theatre. Vaudeville and then the movies. Then they turned it into a roller skating rink when the malls took the business out of the centers of the towns. But they've torn it down now. Now there's just a vacant lot with bare earth. Brown, brown earth. Same color, pretty much, as my own skin. They haven't started digging into it yet to put in the foundation for whatever it is they want the earth to bear the weight of now. I plan to be out of here before they start.

There's a war movie on the television. The television was put in here for the man in the bed next to me. I guess they can charge it off, too, to whatever health insurance is paying for him being here — even if I'm not entirely sure he can understand anything on it. Not that there's that much to understand most of the time. They've got it up perched on a shelf on the wall, like an eagle on a cliff up where it can look down at its prey and swoop for the kill. Sometimes I wish I could turn that television off, but since I don't have a private room, I have no choice but to watch it or try to sleep. But I like to watch movies, even the bad ones. Those are the ones I usually had parts in. I watch, hoping to catch a glimpse of that mythical enemy of all gooks (foreign and domestic), John Wayne. I've always liked John Wayne. He even shared a sandwich with me when I was a Hollywood Indian. We were both young then and didn't know any better. He had a small speaking part in the movie he was in and all I had to do in mine was shoot someone with an arrow and then get shot off a horse myself. I seldom talked in any of the movies they hired me for except for the movie where I played a Mexican. The director didn't think I looked Italian enough to be an Indian.

But the movie on the color TV didn't have John Wayne in it, even though it was made in 1942. It had one scene, though, that I really liked. The Germans have managed to penetrate the American codes. Now a vital message has to be sent by the radio. But the Germans know the secret code. World War II is about to be won by the Germans if the Americans can't get this message out in time. (I smiled then, because I knew what was going to happen.) But wait! There, next to the radio operator, is a Navajo Indian. He takes the mic. The screen splits and on the other side is yet another Navajo holding another microphone. They begin speaking to each other in their Native Indian Language. The scene shifts to the headquarters of Nazi intelligence. They hear the intercepted message. There are confused looks on their faces. They beat their breasts and groan. The new American code is unbreakable! Little do they realize that the ethnic diversity they have so diligently suppressed in Europe is now the key to their defeat at the hands of America and her allies. All over the world black and brown and yellow people (forget, for the moment, the Japanese — honorary Aryans, anyhow) are joining together to defeat the Third Reich. The moment of victory is now at hand — all because of two Navajos.

Two Navajos. The Code Talkers. I lean back and chuckle, remembering World War Two and Wayne Porico.

Wayne Porico was a White Mountain Apache. We went through

basic training together and ended up in the same infantry outfit. Wayne was a big round man with a big sense of humor. Red Prince Number One was what he called himself. I was Red Prince Number Two. He told me how he ended up going to war for the same United States Army which once made a career out of trying to corral various of his relatives while they made a career out of stealing from the Mexicans and eluding the soldiers of two different nations.

As soon as World War Two started, Wayne reported to the Indian Agent on his reservation.

"I have come to enlist," Wayne said.

The Indian Agent was moved. Wayne had a reputation as a troublemaker and was the last person he'd ever expected to be a patriot.

"That is wonderful," the Indian Agent said. "You want to fight against the common enemy?"

"Yup," Wayne said. "I sure do. But there's just one problem."

"What's that?" The Indian Agent said.

"I'm not sure they'll let me enlist in the Japanese Army."

The Indian Agent got so upset at Wayne's joke that he looked like he was about to cry. Wayne always had a soft heart. So he told the Agent he was only kidding. He really did want to enlist in the American Army — even though all he had really intended to do was pull the Indian Agent's leg.

"My goddam Indian sense of humor got me here!" Wayne told me.

Wayne Porico was quite a guy. He loved the desert the way I loved the mountains. It was my lucky day he and I were together when we were dropped in groups of two all over the North African desert.

All we had were the clothes on our backs, knives, rifles, mess kits and a radio. We were supposed to be scouts of some kind — that was how they described our objective. I described our objective as getting back to the base alive. The radio was for us to call them to come and get us when we had gone as far as we could go without help. It ended up with us being the only ones who never used our radio.

After we disentangled ourselves from our chutes, we looked around. I was a little worried, but Wayne thought he was back home.

"Wow," he said, "look at all this great sand, look at those beautiful rocks!"

I didn't say anything. Wayne walked around picking and turning over rocks.

"Oh great!" he said. He bent over to pick up a crooked brown stick which began to move in his hand. He held it up to my face. "Look at the fangs on this one."

"Don't do that," I said. The brown stick was a four foot long snake. Wayne put it back down, but it wasn't long before he found another one.

That desert was crawling with snakes. Either that or Wayne attracted them. I have a Sioux friend who was that way with birds. I once saw a partridge walk right up to him, let him pick it up and ruffle its neck feathers. Wayne was that way with snakes. They liked each other.

"I think this one is some kind of viper," he'd say.

"Just don't get it near me," I'd say.

But before long, I had to let them get near me because that was what we ate. Wayne didn't see anything wrong about killing them and eating them and neither did I about the first part. After a while, I got used to eating them, too. They tasted a little like roasted chicken. Wayne really knew how to cook a snake. By then we had a pretty good routine going. We'd spend the hottest part of the day in whatever shade we could find — sometimes digging ourselves into the sand. During the coldest part of the night, we'd walk. About every third day Wayne would find water to drink.

One night, though, we were kind of tired. We'd walked and jogged maybe forty miles. We lay down and I was asleep as soon as I closed my eyes. Wayne's voice woke me up.

"Foxy," he said, "Just open your eyes, but don't move."

Wayne had his hand on my chest, his whole arm, it felt like. Then I opened my eyes and saw it wasn't Wayne's arm at all. It was a very large black cobra. I blinked my eyes and it stuck out its tongue. Then I heard Wayne start to sing something. I couldn't make out the words, but it made me feel okay, even with the snake on my chest. Before I knew it, I'd closed my eyes again. When I opened them it was dawn. The snake was gone. Wayne was leaning against the rock outcrop we'd sheltered near.

"Red Prince Number Two is sleeping late," he said.

"How the hell did that snake get on me?"

"Crawled up last night. I think it got cold. Snakes'll do that."

"How the hell did you know it was there?"

"It crawled over me first. I guess I wasn't as warm as you are. Good thing you had your shirt buttoned up tight. Uncle of mine once had a rattlesnake crawl right in next to his skin. He didn't like it at all. Snakes got cold skin."

"I didn't like it at all, either."

"No? Well, I could put a circle around us when we sleep. That'd keep the snakes away."

"That works?"

"If you do it right."

"Why the hell didn't you do it before?"

"Gee, Foxy, I never thought one little snake crawling over you would bother you that much."

All in all, Red Prince Number One and Red Prince Number Two made out okay in the North African desert. We even put on weight. The only problem came when we climbed up a sand hill and found ourselves looking down on the base. Wayne wanted to turn around and go back into the desert. It took some talking to convince him to come in.

There had been some Germans out in that desert, too, but we didn't bother them and they didn't see us. When we told our Commander about them and where we'd been seeing them, though, he got pretty excited. Our mission had been a success.

It was that success which gave him his big idea — or maybe he had just seen a certain war movie. He called us in.

"I am assigning you to special communications," he said.

We stood there.

"Each of you will be in a different team."

We still stood there. There wasn't any reason to say anything.

The Commander walked over to the wall where a large map hung. He tapped it with a finger. I recognized the gesture. It had been in that war movie. He must have practiced, because he did it well.

"The Germans," he said, "have broken our code. They can decipher anything we transmit." He smiled. "That is what the Nazis think." He tapped the map again. He was overdoing it. The officer in the movie only did it once. "They do not know about you, though. Whenever we are in a special situation where secret information must be sent from one unit to another, you will come in. The enemy will never be able to decipher your communications." He tapped the map a third time and Wayne looked at me. I shrugged. "They will never be able to understand it because you will speak to each other over the radio in your *Native Indian language.*"

We saluted and left the room.

The problem was, of course, that Wayne was an Apache and I wasn't. I didn't know his language for beans and aside from that year I spent in the mountains with my grandfather when he kidnapped me from the Indian school, my native Indian language had been English.

We worked it out, though. It turned out both of us had taken a course in Basic German in school. Neither one of us had passed, so we figured we were equally fluent. We practiced some and got to the point where we could understand each other real good. And we spoke it so badly that no one else could understand a word we were saying — or even what language we were speaking. We only had that assignment for a couple of months. Then the war ended in North Africa and we were shipped out. But before then I bet we did make a few German intelligence officers who listened in on our conversations beat their breasts and groan.

All Dishonest Men

"Want some, Sam?" Lincoln Baker held out the can of chewing tobacco.

Sam Bowen shook his head. "My Ma wouldn't like it."

"C'mon," Lincoln Baker smiled. He pointed at the war-bonneted Indian painted on the lid. "Mebbe this is one of your relatives?"

Sam Bowen leaned back, brought his right knee up to his chest. Anyone but Linc had said that, he'd of been angry. It was hard to get mad at Linc.

"Them stories ain't so," Sam said, narrowing his eyes as he always did when he was about to say something other than the truth. It made his head ache to lie, but the habit of denying was too deeply ingrained. Folks treat you different if you're not like them. "What some say about us being Indin is just stuff. We's French."

He looked away from Linc towards the Farm-To-Market crossroads. There were few cars today going by the Spiers Falls Store. Some days there were a lot of them, long black ones with two men in front and heavy canvas over the back. Rum-runners like the Heyer brothers. Bringing liquor down from Canada. Even Legs Diamond came down that road sometimes. He'd killed men, but Sam found it hard to believe that Legs Diamond was worse than Big Bill Heyer. Big Bill even stole from the bootleggers, rolling out a keg or two where one of his brothers could pick it up.

Sam remembered the man who came and paid to rent the barn they weren't using. To store hay, he'd said. But when the big truck full of bags of sugar turned down the long dirt road that ended at their little place, Sam's father stopped it.

"No," Jean Bowen said. "The liquor making is not for my farm."

For a minute Sam thought there was going to be a fight. He picked up a rock and held it behind his back, ready to throw, but something in his father's eyes stopped the two men in cloth caps who had climbed halfway out of the truck.

The next day, the man who had rented the barn came back. Jean Bowen handed him back the twenty dollars.

"You count it," he said, "all is there."

The man looked angry. Sam watched out of the corner of his eyes as he whittled at the piece of pine which was turning into a turtle. The man reached for his pocket and Sam saw his father take a deep breath. *Pa's going to do the yell!* Sam thought. But the man only pulled out a handkerchief. The man was sweating hard. Sam and his father were not sweating, but the man from the city was. It was because of the way his father was looking at him.

"You go now," Jean Bowen said. His voice was soft. "You take from my barn the things you placed there. That will be all. My fences will not be cut, my animals will not be shot or poisoned."

The man looked at his father with that look of surprise which Sam had seen before on the face of someone when Jean Bowen seemed to read his thoughts. The man picked up the money from the table, stuffed it into his pocket and walked backwards, his eyes on Sam's father. Jean Bowen did not rise from his chair. He moved his head towards the door, pointing at it with his chin. The man grabbed at the knob and went out. The chair he'd been sitting in was dark from his sweat. They heard his car start and the sounds of its engine grow fainter. Finally Sam could hear it no longer, though his father still sat, head cocked to one side. At last, Jean Bowen turned.

"That chair," he said, "break it into pieces and burn it in the stove."

Though others who'd refused such offers in the past had bought only trouble, none came to the Bowens. The still was set up on another farm off the North Creek Road. Sam learned about it a few months later from the paper. "ILLEGAL STILL BURNS," ran the headline. There had been an accident when the volatile liquid caught fire. The only one hurt was the man who had visited them.

That man, though, hadn't been one of the Heyers. They were worse than that. Sam held up the piece of wood in his hand. The late afternoon light caught the grain. He could almost see a shape in it. Maybe he should take his jackknife out now.

"Sam," Lincoln Baker said, "you see that car go by?"

"Looked t'be a Packard."

"I think I recognized the plate number!"

"Don't you scare yourself! That was all months ago."

"He said he didn't care how long it took, Sam."

Lincoln Baker coughed hard and the tobacco flew out. The brown wad was flecked with blood.

"Dammit, Linc," Sam said. "You oughtn't to be using that stuff. You know your lungs is too weak."

Lincoln Baker wiped his mouth with his handkerchief. "When I was little they said I wouldn't live to be fourteen. I already beat 'em by two years."

Sam clenched his fist. Like his father, his impulse was to fight. But this sickness? How could he fight against that? There were ways to heal people. But with the consumption gone into Linc so deep and for so long? And up to now Sam had never showed an interest in learning the healing ways his father knew. *But mebbe,* he thought.

"Lincoln John Baker," a voice said. It was a flat hard voice like a shovel striking against stone. The black Packard was stopped across the road. Sun glinted from the window half rolled down on the driver's side.

Lincoln Baker stood up. Sam grabbed his arm.

"Dammit, Linc! Don't you go!"

"It ain't no use," Lincoln Baker said. He pulled his arm free with unexpected strength. "It's me they want, Sam. You stay here."

Shading his eyes against the sun with one hand, Linc started across the road. Without hesitation, Sam followed, hearing their feet crunching the gravel as they walked, hearing everything around them as if for the first time: wind in the dry grass, a shrew rustling leaves in the ditch, the pinging of the car's hot engine. Two steps ahead, Lincoln Baker moved like a man without a shadow.

Damn your honest mouth, Linc, Sam thought.

Four months ago Lincoln Baker had been walking home when a wagon pulled up and offered him a ride. It wasn't till he climbed in that he realized it was Big Bill Heyer. They were stopped down the road by the police, but Big Bill jumped off and disappeared in the bushes, leaving Linc alone with a wagon full of stolen furniture. In court, Linc identified him as the man driving. It meant a month in the lock-up for Big Bill Heyer.

"No man ever sent me to jail before," Big Bill Heyer said. "No man ever shall do so again."

Linc's feet brushed against a stink bug on the road. Its thick, sweet smell filled Sam's nose. In front of them, the back door swung open. Upholstery gleamed black as a hearse.

"Get in," the man in back said. He looked at Sam. "You too."

"No," Lincoln Baker said, realizing for the first time that Sam had followed. "Sam, stay here!" But the man's hand reached up and grabbed Linc by the shoulder, pulling him in. All Sam could do was follow.

The door shut, solid and smooth. It seemed final to Sam, as if it were the last door either of them would ever hear. Not another living soul had seen them leave. Old Seneca Smith was in the store drowsing behind the dry goods counter. No one else had been out front or on the road. The men in the car chose their time well. And there wouldn't be much fuss about the disappearance of two boys from poor families.

Linc's ma is never going to forgive me for letting this happen to him, Sam thought. Then, suddenly, he thought of his own mother, his sisters, his father.

The man in the back seat with them said nothing, but he was smiling. The smile said enough. The driver drove without looking back or asking directions. He knew where they were going.

"I'm sorry, Sam," Lincoln Baker said. "I've got you killed, too." On the other side of Linc, Big Bill Heyer still smiled. Sam looked up at the rearview mirror. The driver's face reflected in it wore the same hard smile. It was the same calm look Sam had seen in the eyes of two dogs he'd surprised in the woods as they were creeping up on a fawn. *Damn,* he thought, *you two think you're something.*

"Can't you just leave my friend be?" Lincoln Baker said. "He won't say nothing."

Big Bill Heyer pressed the muzzle of his gun hard against Lincoln Baker's knee. "Shuddup, boy. You and your friend is going for a ride. We thought you'd like to see the falls."

Sam tried to speak. He wanted to tell Linc not to worry. They only wanted to frighten him. This was broad daylight. This was 1925, for God's sake. But he could say nothing. He knew what Big Bill Heyer would do. In the trunk of the car would be rope and weights, maybe even some buckets and dry cement to hold their feet like heavy grey boots, their feet sunk into stone. Feet sunk into stone.

"Aw-haw," his father said. "You want to hear that story again?"

"Yes," Sam and his sisters said.

"One day Old Sabattis, he went into town. He bought the things he needed at the store. Then he sat down to wait on the corner. By and by, some of the white men who loafed around there came up. First they pretended to do a war dance around him. Then they start taunting him.

'Hey Chief,' they said, 'do somethin' for us.'

But the old man just sit on the curb, ignoring them.

'Come on, Chief, do some magic for us.'

But still Sabattis, he pay them no mine.

Then one a them pull back his foot to kick the old man. . ."

Something shook Sam's arm. It was Link coughing. "Sam," he said between coughs, "I'm so sorry."

"It's all right, Linc," Sam said.

The gun slid in between them, pushing them apart.

"By Christ," Bill Heyer growled, "I mean to have you silent."

Linc coughed again and Sam slid his hand into his pocket, feeling the familiar metal. The car was going down the hill now. The falls were close.

But the old man stood up. He began to walk towards the men who had been taunting him, holding out his hands. Their faces go pale as he walks, for his feet sink into the stones of the street with each step, his face is like the demon, or the lugaroo. Then he open his mouth and scream!

Sam breathed in deeply. He filled his chest with the memory of those things his father had taught him to hear: the harsh moan of the wind in winter, the scream of the bobcat from the forest on a moonless night, the hunting cry of the owl which freezes the blood of those about to feel the killing claws. Then, as the old man had done, Sam screamed. He screamed the m'teoulin's yell his father taught him, the scream which stops the breath and the heart.

The whole car seemed to vibrate. The driver grabbed his ears and Big Bill Heyer yelled as the car swerved over the shoulder and began to go down the embankment.

The gun had fallen from Heyer's hand. Sam grabbed at it with his right hand. With his left he pulled out the knife he'd opened inside his pocket tearing the cloth of his own pants. He stabbed it at the big man's arm. The knife bit in, but Sam missed the gun as Linc's shoulder slammed into him. The car was bouncing wildly as it went down the hill. The man in front had the wheel again, trying to bring it back under control. The three in the back seat were thrown against the door of the car and Big Bill Heyer's gun thundered, filling the air with the bitter smell of cordite. Sam slashed backhanded with his knife. It cut across the big tendons in Bill Heyer's wrist. The gun fell to the floor as Big Bill Heyer grabbed at his arm where blood spurted like water from a rusty pump. Then a tree leaped up, filling the windows of the car.

Sam didn't know how long his eyes were closed. Perhaps no more than a moment. He opened them. Bill Heyer's eyes were staring straight at him. But the face was upside down, the head strangely dented in. Sam pushed the dead face away from him and the car, which was on its side, rocked slightly. Every part of his body hurt.

"Linc?" he said. He shoved Heyer's body aside, ignoring the way it made the car shift, gravel whispering beneath metal. He grabbed Lincoln Baker's arm and pushed back against the door above him. It creaked open and Sam levered himself through, dragging Linc with him. He lay there for a time looking up at the sky. There were dark clouds overhead. *It's going to rain,* he thought.

The car was balanced close to the edge of the cliff above the falls. Sam tried to stand, one arm still around Linc. Then he saw the driver. The dark glasses hung from one ear and his right eye was filled with blood. The driver's shoulder was at a strange angle and he leaned against the car as if he could not stand without its support. It was Jim Heyer, Big Bill Heyer's brother. He was holding a cut-off shotgun.

Sam stood. He looked straight at Jim Heyer, his gaze steady. The gun pointed at his chest began to waver and Jim Heyer's one eye glazed with something which was not anger. Jim Heyer shook his head and began to push at the earth with both his feet, as if trying to run backwards. But the car was at his back and he could move no further. Then slowly, so slowly it seemed a dream, the car and Jim Heyer went over the cliff. Sam stepped forward, but the car and Jim Heyer were gone.

Sam turned back to Linc. Linc's eyes were open.

"We beat 'em, Sam." Lincoln Baker coughed as he tried to

breathe in. The blood at the edges of his mouth was frothy. His voice came out as a whisper Sam had to lean close to hear. "And I beat 'em all by a good two years."

Sam looked at Lincoln Baker's hand. The fingers relaxed, and Sam could see that Linc had still been holding the can of tobacco. The first drops of rain tapped a slow drum beat on the Indian head on its cover. For just a moment, before his own eyes filled, Sam saw his own face reflected back from the film of water on top of the metal face.

"Damn," Sam said. "Damn all dishonest men."

Wolves

Louis Lawless never knew for sure who it was who claimed to have killed the last wolf, but he knew — as did everyone else in the county — that it was Danny-Boy Stoner's father, Old Stoner, who did in the last panther. The story the mean-eyed old man told was that it was crouched on top of Devil's Rock, tail switching side to side, about to leap on him. "Eyes red as sin with the Devil's own light," Old Stoner said. "Jes managed to get the gun up in time. Shot it right between them eyes."

That was decades ago, and Old Stoner had been dead for ten years, but Danny-Boy still told that panther tale to anyone he could corner in front of the town post office. Danny-Boy, who was fifty-two years old, had wild animals on his mind. There were rumors of a wolf in the mountain range that girdled the northern edge of the small Vermont town like a giant's eyebrow. A timber wolf bigger than a German Shepherd. It was Danny-Boy's opinion that it needed getting rid of. Some of those in the town thought it was the other way around, but, aside from Louis Lawless, they didn't say it out loud.

Danny-Boy still had his hair cut in the sandy-haired flat-top he wore in high school in the 50's. He was a lantern-jawed and gaunt 6'4" with sloping shoulders and fists the size of small melons. There was a plate in his head from a car accident, but it hadn't slowed down his weekend progress from one bar room brawl to another or his appearances in the town court every month or so. Town Justice Allen was almost fond of Danny-Boy. "One of my regulars," he called him. Mean as he was when he was drunk, Danny-Boy Stoner was worse when he was sober. Sober, he was cunning enough to know what it meant to a man when Danny-Boy confronted him the week before a court appearance to tell him how nice his wife was dressing now and how Danny-Boy wondered if anybody would ever take it into their head to come and visit a pretty woman like that when her husband wasn't home.

Danny-Boy had no worries about money. Though he'd worked

for years in the garage at the Mobil station as an assistant mechanic, he'd been self-sufficient for the last few years after inheriting a chunk of money and a good piece of property from his father when Old Stoner was killed in the car accident. Everybody knew that when Danny-Boy sold it to the Snowflake Development Group, he'd be a rich man. Snowflake had been trying to buy it from Old Stoner before he died, but the old man had vowed that he'd die before he'd sell out. And that, everyone agreed before the car accident, was likely to be a long ways down the road. Even though the old man had been in his nineties, there was talk at the Post Office before his decease that Dan Stoner wasn't never going to die. He'd grown short and thinner with age, but was still as hard as a piece of knotted wood. Regular as death and taxes, he drove his car into town each morning to sit in front of the store. Tourists passing through the town, having taken a wrong turn on their way to another, better-marked place, would see him and think of him as the typical New Englander. Fortunately for most, they seldom stopped to talk to the quaint old man or ask him directions. Old Stoner's vocabulary for flatlanders was limited but colorful. He hadn't been a well-liked man, but he was a part of the landscape of the town and that sort of familiarity leads to tolerance, especially after age has worn away some of the rough edges — or at least blurred the memories of those whose grudges were held the hardest.

Old Stoner had outlived most of his enemies with the exception of "The Indian" —Theo Lawless. In his heyday Old Stoner had been as little-loved and as feared as Danny-Boy. A smaller man than his son, Old Stoner had preferred to use other methods than fists to even scores he counted against himself. Perhaps the only reason Theo was still around was that Stoner was not as good a shot as he set himself up to be unless he could sneak up on a man's back. Try as he might, Old Daniel Stoner had never been able to get close enough in the woods to Theo Lawless to get a clear shot. More than once, though, Theo had heeded an inner voice which told him to duck, heard a bullet cut the leaves above his head and then heard the far-off *PWAP!* of a familiar small-calibre rifle. Woodsman though he prided himself on being, Old Stoner never found the cabin which everyone knew The Indian had in the Black Rock Range.

The enmity between Old Stoner and The Indian was a natural one. Stoner was a trapper and a woodsman of the kind people called "a game hog." He prided himself on always knowing whatever the limit was so he could double it. Anything he could get in his sights was "in season." Theo Lawless had been the county game warden and took his job as Game Protector seriously. Every citation for violating the game laws and every fine levied against Old Stoner had been a result of Theo's vigilance.

It was not that Theo was a hard man or in love with the law. He looked the other way when a poor family found it necessary to get some "woodland veal" by shooting a deer out of season. In fact, though road-killed deer were taken by the county jails in most parts of the state, somehow the state police could never get to those roadkills fast enough in Theo's county. The state road was a main route for the big trucks heading downstate and at certain times of year there might be as many as three deer killed every week on that road. Theo was there before the animal had cooled off and the only evidence of an animal's death would be the bloodstain on the road and a handful of tobacco from his Prince Albert can left where its head had lain. Theo did the same for any animal killed on the road. Some said it was the only thing religious about the man, though there were others who failed to see anything religious at all about it. The poor families in the hills around town saw no reason to complain, for the venison from those deer always ended up in their larders. And up in the hills, where there was more Indian blood than any of the families would own up to, there were some who said that everything Theo Lawless did was religious.

It was Theo Lawless who pointed out, in a quiet voice, that the panther which Old Daniel Stoner shot must have been doing a somersault when it attacked. The only bullet hole, he said, was in the back of its head. He leaned over to point at the animal's foot where Stoner had dropped it on the front porch of the store. "And this surely does look like the mark of a steel trap."

Daniel Stoner — who was in his thirties back then — took a swing at Theo with the butt of his rifle. Theo stepped aside, faded back like a gust of wind, and that swing of Stoner's carried the trapper right on through the window of the general store. The trip to the doctors to get his arm sewed back up — it took thirty stitches — had considerably soured Old Dan's victory that day on bringing in a dangerous beast and collecting the bounty. It was a year to the day after that when Theo

Lawless took his oath and put on his game protector's badge for the first time.

Over the years, something close to grudging respect developed between the two men. Or at least there was enough respect on Stoner's side for him never to carry his quarrel with The Indian any further than the man himself. Lawless's wife and family went unmolested. Which was probably just as well for Stoner. Everyone agreed that Old Stoner was a tough man. Tough enough to chew nails and spit tacks, they said when they talked about him down at the general store. Tough as a bulldog and just as ornery. So tough that when he got bit by a timber rattler on the little finger of his left hand he'd killed the snake first and then just pulled out his knife and lopped that finger right off. But tough as Old Stoner was, everyone agreed that they'd rather have Stoner mad at them than Theo Lawless. The Indian was a quiet enough man, but there was something about the way he walked which made the voices of other people become less loud when they noticed he was around. And no one spoke of Theo Lawless as "The Indian" when he was anywhere to be seen.

Calling a man an Indian was kin to deadly insult in a county where being known to be Native meant, within living memory, being open to the deadliest forms of prejudice. The people of that hill county who were of Indian blood knew who they were and they knew their neighbors knew who they were. That unspoken knowledge was enough and there was a line there not to be crossed. Crossing it in public could lead to a killing. And it was stated clearly enough in the history books that the Indians had never really lived in that county — or anywhere in the state for that matter. They'd only been passing through, as it were. And the last of them, officially, had passed through in 1898. Town records mentioned four Indian families trying to set up tents to camp along the river bed for a summer in that same year the last wolves were brought in for the bounty to the county seat. The four Indian families had been ridden out of town on a rail.

From that date on, in the birth records of that county seat, those of Indian blood were listed as being "French" or "Canadian." With the exception of the Lawless family. It said "Indian" on Theo Lawless' birth records — just as it did on Louis' own birth certificate, when he was born fifty years after his great-uncle. Though Old Daniel Stoner's best known ancestor had been a famous killer of Indians in the 1700's and the county records listed him as white, there was also enough Native blood in his veins for the word Indian to appear after his name as well. No county clerk who wanted to keep walking would have dared to put that word on the birth record of any Stoner. "There's no worse Indian hater than an Indian who hates himself," Theo Lawless said to his nephew.

Louis Lawless sat up in bed.

"What's wrong?" Annie said. She put the warm palm of her right hand against the side of his face and grasped his left wrist with her other hand. His hand wasn't shaking, though, as it did when he woke up with the night sweats, seeing the side of Jimmy Baptiste's head explode like a coconut when the bullet hit it.

"Uncle Theo," he said. There was a calmness in his voice she hadn't heard since his return from the fighting in Central America, since the last job he'd had to quit because his hands started shaking again and he started seeing the faces of dead men. "He's come back."

"I'll make coffee," Annie said. Her own family was Mohawk, from Akwesasne. It was a family that knew something about dreams. She slipped on her robe and went out the door into the trailer's narrow hall.

Louis slid over to her side of the bed and swung his feet onto the cold floor. He leaned forward to look out the window. The street light illuminated the edge of the autumn woods, the woods of the Black Rock Range which began to rise just behind their lot, Lot #13. "That's a good number for us," Uncle Theo said on the day they moved the trailer in. "Same number as plates on a turtle's back. Same number as moons in a year. Good lot number for a Lawless." Uncle Theo stayed on with them for three months, coming into the bedroom to put his hand on Louis's brow when the nightsweats began, holding him down when the noise of the sniper fire got so loud in his ears again all he could see were the shattered streets of the city, all he could smell was blood and burning bone, all he could feel was the bullet hitting him in the shoulder, then the rumble of the dust-off choppers coming in.

"You're out there," Louis said. "Thank God, you're out there." He leaned his forehead against the windowpane and turned his head to the right. Theo's shotgun hung there on the wall. He reached out his right hand and wiped a small flecking of dust from the black steel.

As he sat in the kitchenette of the trailer he made circles on the top of the table with the moist base of his coffee cup. Annie waited. Louis took a deep breath. "It was so good to see him," he said. "He was behind that old cabin of his. I could see it clear as day, even though I haven't been there since I was seven. There were pens behind the cabin. I'd never seen them there before. And he was opening them up and all kinds of animals were coming out of them. As they came out, they'd dance around him, like a round dance, you know. Like they was greeting him. And he was just nodding to them. Bears, wolves, lions, all of them greeting him and then going back into the woods. Then he saw me and he called me over and I was with him in the midst of all of those animals."

Annie put her hand on his again.

"He said it was my turn now. My turn to take care of them. To take care of our people."

The boy was four years old when they brought him to Theo.

"Just for a while, Uncle Theo," they said.

Theo nodded. It had been too long since he and Millie had children around. There was space. And the boy had his head up and didn't look like a kicked dog. Louis. Looo-wee. If he was to go to the county home and then to foster parents he'd be learning soon enough to look down towards the earth as the only safe place to put his eyes. Not to look up as he did now, up like a hawk looking to take flight into the sun.

Louis stayed. He stayed through grade school. He stayed after Aunt Millie passed when he was twelve years old. Weekends and vacations he spent by Theo's side, walking the trails or riding the hill and mountain roads in the green Game Protector's truck. He learned as much from the old man's silence as he did from his words.

When he was six, Theo brought him a dog. They named her Malsum. Wolf. She was grey and rangy, big like no other dog in the town and some wondered where Theo had gotten that pup. Not from the county pound or from any of the farms around. Louis was eleven when the Stoner boy spun his wheel part way up on their lawn and hit Malsum with his front bumper. The dog flew through the air like a clod of earth kicked up by a horse's hoof. The milk truck was taking a turn from the Windsor place two houses down or the Stoner boy wouldn't have stopped. But he had to and his car stalled after he hit the brakes.

Louis knelt by the dog. The Stoner boy got out of the car. He was not a boy, even though everyone called him that. He was 38 years old, a Marine Corps tattoo on his left bicep. He rolled his dirty T-shirt sleeve up to hold his cigarettes and expose the words in bleeding red. Semper Fi. He'd never been in the corps. Flat feet had kept him out when he was drafted for Vietnam. But he got the tattoo a year later. Over "Semper Fi" were the words "Big Dan." It was what he wanted to be called. But no one called him that. Everyone called him Danny-Boy because his father was the real Dan Stoner. Anyone who said "Danny-Boy" within his hearing would feel a hand on his shoulder, and turn to find one of those big fists heading for his face. Danny specialized in sucker punches.

Uncle Theo was on his way from across the road. He'd been over to the store and came out at the sound of the screeching brakes.

"That goddamn dog of yours," the Stoner boy mouthed, standing in the middle of the road. "Run right out in front of me. I hope the hell I killed the goddamn bitch."

Theo Lawless went to step around the bigger man, who loomed over him like Goliath. Danny-Boy sidestepped and put himself between the old man and the boy bent over the dog.

"You keep that goddamn kid out the road or I'll by God run him over, too."

Theo Lawless reached out one hand and pushed Danny-Boy Stoner aside. He did it as effortlessly as if the bigger man weighed nothing. Danny-Boy took a stumbling step and then spun fast on his heel. His right fist clubbed down towards the back of Theo's head. But the head was no longer there when his fist reached that spot. The old man had dropped to one knee. Then, rising up the way a partridge bursts up out of cover, Theo straightened and swung his cupped hand against the big man's ear. It popped like a rifle shot and Danny-Boy dropped like a poll-axed ox. Blood flowed out of his burst ear as he lay on the ground bellowing. His father, passing by just then in his red Chevy Truck, pulled over and climbed out, dragged his son to his feet.

"The old bastard hit me with a hammer, Paw," Danny-Boy blubbered.

Old Stoner threw a quick glance towards the road edge where Theo Lawless was moving his hands along the grey dog's body. Millie Lawless was standing there, too, holding something long in her hands. Old Stoner blinked. The old woman was holding a 12 guage shotgun.

Old Stoner shook his head.

"Get in the truck, you bawling baby. He may be an old bastard and half your size, but he's twice the man you'll never be."

Louis heard those words and saw the look which answered them in Danny-Boy's eyes. He'd seen the look first when he was ten and Theo had taken him to a small traveling circus. They were walking through the tent where the animals were kept when they came upon a trainer poking at a big caged chimpanzee with a stick. The look in the animal's eyes held a sort of hatred Louis had never seen before.

Theo noticed it, too. "One day," the old man said, "he will kill that man, stick or no stick."

Though her hip was broken, Malsum recovered. And Danny-Boy Stoner kept his distance from both Theo and Louis. There seemed to be no thought in his mind to try to get back at Theo for breaking his eardrum. Theo waited for the sheriff or the state police to come to their home, but Danny-Boy never filed a complaint. Louis understood why. After Old Stoner's death many years later, Louis thought back to that look on Danny-Boy's face, the blood reddening his hand as he climbed into that truck with his father. Danny-Boy had transferred all of his anger to the father who shamed him.

It was an anger only held in check by fear. Old Stoner kept a peeled hickory pole behind his chair to maintain what he called "godly order" in his home. Old Stoner's wife had left her husband because of that godly order. She took her bruises and went to live with an unmarried sister in Montpelier when Danny-Boy was twelve. Her fear of her husband's daily beatings had left no time in her life to show love for their son. Though Danny-Boy hated his father, his contempt for his mother was greater. When the impulse to flee finally came upon her like the sudden sound of thunder from a winter sky and she ran, Danny-Boy refused to go with her. Instead, as she stumbled down the dirt road to stop the green truck heading past their lane, still holding the dish she'd been drying in her right hand and the dish towel in her left, Danny-Boy hurried into the woods to find his father out following the trapline.

"Maw's run off, Pa. If you hurry you might catch her," were his words when he found his father on the beaver dam trail. But instead of chasing his wife, Daniel Stoner sat down and took out his buck knife.

"Take this and cut you a good strong sapling. Peel it and bring it to me," were his grim words. And Danny-Boy did as he said, already feeling the stick whistle and cut across his own bare back as he lopped it.

That day when Danny-Boy followed his father into the woods was the last time he ever entered the forest when his old man was there. Perhaps on another occasion Old Daniel Stoner might have been kinder to his son. But not that day. All along the line, every trap he'd set had been empty. And there was no good explanation for it. The news that his useless woman had finally left him with one less mouth to feed had bothered him less than his son coming upon him with his pack basket empty. It was the shame of his failure that he cut into Danny-Boy's back with every stroke. Perhaps his anger towards his wife would have been greater if he had known that the one who ended up giving her the ride down to the one spot in the county where she would get that Montpelier bus was his old enemy, Theo Lawless in his green game protector's truck.

Nights, especially when the days were short and the snow on the ground, Theo liked to talk. Tell stories or just talk, mostly about the animals. It seemed as if he had a special story for every animal in the forest. The ones who were no longer there seemed to be his favorites. He spoke of them the way another man might speak of close and well-loved relatives moved away to another country. That was the way he talked about the wolves.

"Wolves take good care of their families," he said. "A man could do worse than to be like a wolf. They protect their own and they don't forget. They stay loyal to their mates all their lives. If they lose their mate, they might just die of sorrow. Up in Canada one time, I came across a female wolf in a trap. Just her paw was caught and it was turned around so she couldn't get at it to gnaw it off, gnaw herself free. Her mate was there right next to her, not caught in the trap, but staying there with her. Bringing her food. Trap probably hadn't been checked in a week. You know, if a man's got to run a line of traps, he's got a duty to those animals he's trying to catch to check that line every day. It's one thing to expect them to give their lives, but it's another to expect them to suffer longer than's needed. I don't hold with a man who doesn't check his traps regular."

Theo leaned back and looked up at the beams in the ceiling. They were hand-hewn, chestnut. Cut by his own father in building that small old house. Louis and Millie sat in the dark room, sharing the silence as Theo sat there for a time with his memory before speaking it. His chair creaked as he leaned forward towards the pot-belly stove.

"When I opened that trap," he said, "the old man wolf just watched me, like he understood. And the old woman wolf, she just laid there when I worked at it. I don't know if she lost that foot or not. It looked bad, but she limped off and he was right by her side. They didn't look back at all, but they didn't have to."

Theo picked up the poker, opened the door and rearranged a log inside the stove. "A man could do worse than to be a wolf."

"I always knowed he wasn't really dead," Louis said. "That's why they looked but they never found him." He hefted the ashwood packbasket up over his shoulders. "I know where I got to go. He showed me how to find his cabin again in the dream. Or maybe I just remembered it because the dream showed me where to find it again in my memory. That'd be more like what my psychology professor at the Community College would say, eh?" Louis laughed.

Annie smiled again, one of those small smiles that Louis loved the best, just at the edges of her mouth. Too much smiling the way some of the white folks in town smiled would make big wrinkles on a woman's face. That was what her grandmother taught her. She handed Louis the bag with the sandwiches in it.

"Two cans of Doctor Pepper in there," she said. "One's for you. The other one's for Uncle Theo."

"You know, darlin'," Louis smiled, "maybe you could help me a little while I'm gone — look up the dates again for that Civil Service exam. You can't get a job as a Game Warden unless you pass that exam."

Annie opened up the screen door. The wind came to her face from the east, rattling the dry leaves of the oaks. "No sign of snow coming, Chingachook," she said. "Just watch out for wild Indians."

It had been bothering him since he woke up, that dream in which he saw the old man's mean eyes looking out from a wolf's face. As he hung in that space between waking and dreaming, he knew he'd heard the sounds of a wolf howling. He crumpled the third beer can and sent it spinning across the room to join the pile in the corner where a stack of *Hustler* magazines with creased and torn covers were haphazardly tossed. He thought back to what he had said that morning in front of the post office, vowing to find the wolf and kill it, after telling the story of his father's panther for the thousandth time.

Danny-Boy walked across to the fireplace and took down the rifle which hung there. His father's gun, the gun of Old Dan Stoner. It looked real good with the new banana clip he'd got for it. About ten times as many shots as the old magazine. Ordered from the *Soldier of Fortune.* That gun was one of the few things left him that he'd cared for better than the old man had. The new Bronco he'd bought with the insurance money from the accident that wrecked his father's ancient truck and. . . taken the old man's life . . . it already looked to be in worse shape than his father's twenty year old Chevy. Driving off the roads half-drunk and scraping against trees took a toll on even a new vehicle.

Danny-Boy grabbed three boxes of cartridges out of the dresser. He was a good shot, better than his father had been. Each year he killed a dozen or more deer on the range and he'd gotten good enough to shoot the head off of a partridge at fifty yards, kill a squirrel just by hitting the bark right under its feet. He didn't have any use for the taste of wild game and left it laying. He ate his meals at the new fast-food place out on the state road west of town. But he used up plenty of shells practicing and there was nothing better to practice on than moving targets.

He'd go up and follow his father's old trapline. He had a sack of chicken and fries and he could sit in his heavy coat wearing his heavy-sole waterproof boots up there on a ridge for hours without feeling the cold. He'd never felt the cold that much, even as a kid when the old man would chase him out of the house and he'd hide under the foundation in the narrow place where the old bastard couldn't reach him. He opened the refrigerator and took out the last six-pack of Bud and jammed it into the plastic bag with the food.

Danny-Boy slammed the door behind him as he went out. It bounced back from the frame and the doorknob struck him in the small of the back, almost knocking him off the steps. He didn't turn around. Instead he finished loading the gun. Then, twenty paces across the yard he turned around and fired four shots into the door. The fourth shot sent the knob spinning off into the rotting stack of rough lumber piled by the foundation. Danny-Boy smiled and turned back towards the trees, slipping shells into the magazine as he went.

Louis leaned back against the trunk of the ridge-top pine breathing hard. It had been too long since he'd walked so far, so fast, and so high. The town was far below, hidden by the fold of the hills. The sun was three fingers high above the eastern ridge. He thought about the six months which had passed since Theo Lawless had walked into the woods and never come out again. A strong, warm wind from the south dried the sweat on his forehead. He thought about the search parties which had not found him. He thought of the words Uncle Theo said to him on an autumn day like this one four years ago.

"One of these days, Louis, I'm just going to take a long walk and not come back. There won't be no need to come looking for me — unless I call you. You understand?"

"Three more hilltops," Louis said to the wind and to himself. He began walking down the side of the ridge away from the town, the side towards the sun.

Danny-Boy planned to follow the dirt road as far as he could. Then he'd take to the old logging road up behind the little shack where his father lived for his last twenty years, too mean to want to live close to other human beings and too goddam stubborn to die and give Danny-Boy what was rightly his. Wouldn't even lend his son money when he needed it to go into town, even though he could have had plenty by selling off his four hundred acres of land on the mountain to the Snowflake Group. Snowflake was a Condominium and resort developer. If they got this mountain and ran it through the wheels of the various county agencies — which even in this ass-backwards environmental bullshit state, Danny thought, could be made to turn a lot faster when they greased those wheels with money — got the right permits to clear cut them slopes, this place could be like Stowe or Killington. Danny-Boy understood that kind of politics and he wasn't so dumb that he was going to take the offers they were making him now for the mountain. He knew they was in a hurry to get the land. If they had to wait another year, the state would put through the appropriations bill to buy the land and make it part of a state park. But there was no way Danny-Boy was going to sell to the state. Shit! When he sold it, he'd sell it for enough to do exactly what he wanted for the rest of his life. He'd waited long enough for it. Shit, that old bastard didn't ever want to die.

Danny-Boy stopped and looked off the edge of the road. The scars from where the wheels of the red truck went over the edge were long gone now, washed away by more than twenty seasons and the repair work of the town crews. Damn truck went down a fifty foot drop, rolled twice and the old bastard still wasn't killed. Just lucky he'd followed to make sure that cutting the brake line would work. And there he was, crawling up the slope, his mouth full of blood, with a goddamn broken leg. Had to hit him twice with a big rock before he was goddamn dead. Shit.

Danny-Boy knelt to look at the loose sand and gravel at the edge of the road. The tracks looked like those of a big dog. They began further down the slope, down from close to that same rock he'd dropped after braining his father. He finished his second beer, crumpled the can, and threw it down the slope. It bounced off the rock with a ping.

Louis broke off a small piece of his sandwich. He placed it on the ground by the base of the cedar tree.

"Come and share this with me," he said. He'd forgotten to do that when he was in Central America. Sometimes he forgot to do it when he was home inside the trailer. But never when he was eating outdoors, sitting on the earth. It was easy then to remember to share your food with the Little People.

He leaned back against the cedar. "Two more hilltops," he said. He took a bite of the sandwich.

The three-wheeler was where he'd left it, covered over by the tarp in back of his father's old shack. Danny-Boy checked the tank and topped it off with gas. The wolf tracks were all around the shack, circling it and then heading straight up the middle of the log road. He'd follow on the three-wheeler up till the end of the road where the cliffs started. Then he'd get off and walk. He'd discovered years ago that for some reason the deer and the other animals in the forest didn't get spooked by the sound of a trail machine as long as it wasn't right up on their asses. Shit, there were times when he'd be running a chain saw and a deer would come down off the hill just to see what the noise was about.

He tied the pack to the back of the trail machine with bungi cord and slung the rifle over his back. One kick and the motor growled into life. He drained the last Bud, spun gravel in a wheelie and roared up the trail.

Louis leaned against the beech tree which stood at the top of the third hill. His lungs no longer burned from the exertion and his calves no longer hurt. He'd walked through it and come out the other side. He was remembering now, remembering the way old Theo told him it was possible to remember in the woods. Every rock and every tree was in his memory and he felt his footsteps falling exactly into those his uncle had taken. Things were as he remembered them, the sights, the smell, even the sounds. Aside from the distant roar of a trail bike drifting over from the direction of the town, there was nothing to be seen or heard which was different from when Theo brought him this way the last time. He was eighteen. It was one year before he started at the community college to study environmental management. Two years before he enlisted in the Marines. He couldn't say why he'd done that now. Maybe it was because his father had been a Marine when he died in Korea. Near someplace called Chosen. Or because Theo had been a Marine in World War II. Whatever the reason, it had seemed like a good idea at the time.

Louis slid his hand along the tree trunk. The way he'd seen Uncle Theo do it that day as the old man looked out over the roll of mountains and nodded his head towards them.

"Doesn't matter what it says on a deed," Theo Lawless said, "this land doesn't belong to people. Belongs to itself and the best we can do is to care for it. This was all cut over a hundred years ago. Now it's growed back. Forests like these, the animals are coming back into them. There's moose twenty miles north of here, past the second notch. And the lions will be coming back if they'll let them alone."

"And the wolves?" Louis said.

Theo put his hand on the young man's shoulder. "Wolves taught us how to be good scouts," he said. "How to follow a trail and how to watch the enemy without them knowing they was being watched, how to leave a trail to lead them in the wrong direction. It was up in these hills that our old people made their stand. Old Wawanogit —y'know, that means "The One who throws 'em off the track" — and his young warriors used to pass on this trail right through here over two centuries ago on their way down to raid the settlements. They'd hardly have to fire a shot. Just creep up close at night and let out one yell and then fade back into the woods. Next day, those folks would head back south. They wasn't about to mess around with Wawanogit — though that wasn't what they called him. Greylock, was the name they called him. La Tete Blanche, "The Old Whitehead," is what they called him in French. He's what kept them from settling this land so thick like they did down in Connecticut and Massachusetts. Only the loggers come up here and that was a hundred years after Wawanogit walked back into these hills and was never seen again. He was about a hundred years old then, himself. Went off by himself like an old wolf does when his time came to no longer be seen by the people."

A red-tail hawk drifted past them, floating on a thermal which rose from the valley below. It banked as it went by, level with their eyes, almost close enough to touch. It circled higher and higher, its tail an arc of flame. Just before the sight of it was lost in the mid-day sun it called once, a long whistle which drifted down to them.

"The wolves," Theo said, "don't have to return. They never left. Our old people don't leave us."

Danny-Boy Stoner rubbed his ankle and cussed. It wasn't broken, but it sure as hell didn't feel right. He looked down at the three-wheeler thirty feet below, jammed in between two beech trees. There wasn't any use in turning it back over and trying to get it back up onto the trail. The fork was bent at an angle, the tank busted. He stood up and gingerly put weight on his ankle. Didn't seem to be sprained. He could walk on it. Lucky he'd rolled off the bike when those deer came bursting out of the brush. Like they'd been herded right into his path.

He bent over to pick up his gun. As he did, he thought he saw something out of the corner of his eye. He turned quickly to look. Nothing there — or at least nothing more than the faintest hint of a grey shadow vanishing in the witchhobble. He held the gun by the barrel and used it like a cane to limp over to the uphill slope where he thought he'd seen that motion. Where the deer had come leaping out, four of them. So close that one went right over his bike and he had to twist the handlebars so hard to keep from running into the big doe that stopped in his path that the bike went over, pinwheeling down the steep slope. He bent to look, already knowing what he'd find. There were the tracks of the leaping deer. And there, crossing over those tracks, the marks of the wolf. The same as before. There was no mistaking the print of that crippled front paw.

Louis looked down from the last hilltop. He went over and sat on the thick moss which covered the sloping stone of the hilltop edge which faced south west. The sun was in the middle of the sky and as he lay back and closed his eyes, it was warm on his face as if it were still mid-August.

A sound came into his ears and he sat up and opened his eyes. There was a different sort of light in the air and the trees and bushes around him seemed changed, though the moss and the sloping face of stone beneath him were as they had been when he closed his eyes.

Then they were there. A group of men dressed in clothing which fit them as an animal's skin fits it. One of the men wore a hat with two tall feathers stuck into the band and the band itself had a large silver starburst fastened to the front of it. Some of the men carried bows and quivers of arrows, others had long rifles, which he recognized to be muzzle-loaders. The elderly man who led them, the one with the tall-feathered hat, looked familiar. His face was like Theo's, though he was taller, thinner, and the lines of care in his cheeks were deep. They stopped where the trail passed below him, no more than two paces away. Then the leader turned and looked at Louis. He squinted his eyes as he did so, as if trying to see something in the dark, or something obscured by mist. He stepped forward, took something from a pouch at his side and placed it on the moss. Then he stepped back, held out his right hand to gesture down the trail towards the north. He shook his hand four times, and turned back to the others. All of them continued down the trail, passing out of sight behind a huge boulder.

Louis watched them, but he felt no urge to stand and follow them. There was nothing strange about them. He felt as if he had expected to see them, just forgotten it until they came into sight. And now he felt tired. He lay back and closed his eyes again.

When he sat up again he could see from the position of the sun that only a little time had passed. He put his arms back into the straps of his pack. As he did so, he saw there in the moss in front of him, point down, an arrowhead. It looked as if it had been there a long time, for the moss had partially grown over it. He wondered why he hadn't seen it when he sat down. Perhaps it was the angle he was at. It had been shot here on the end of an arrow so long ago that the wood and sinew wrapping had decayed away. He touched the arrowhead with his hand, but didn't pick it up. Things like that were not meant to be picked up — except in your memory. It was good to know it was there.

When he stepped back down onto the trail he looked at the loose earth, expecting to see footprints of some kind. Why? He wasn't sure. But they were there. Louis touched the edge of one of the tracks with his finger. A bit of dirt crumbled into the pad mark. The tracks had been made during that short period when his eyes were closed. They had passed while he was sleeping, perhaps as many as half a dozen of them. Wolves.

He walked a short way north down the trail which led in the direction of Theo's old cabin, the one hidden within a fold in the hills like a boat harbored in a secret cove. But after only a few paces, he shook his head, as if remembering something. He turned off the trail and began to cut across through the brush, making the half circle which a deer makes when it wants to look back along its trail and see what is following it. He climbed a small knoll which overlooked the trail and eased his way into the concealment of the lower branches of a balsam fir. He squatted down by the tree to wait. As he did so he caught the pungent smell and looked at the base of the tree. One of the wolves, probably the oldest, had urinated there, marking the edge of its territory. He smiled, remembering Theo telling him about the way wolves marked their territory. He had been eleven then and they were on the south trail which led past Devil's Rock.

"Thing about a wolf," Theo said, "is that it pays attention to its own territory. Knows where its own range is and don't stray into someone else's. Wolves give each other respect. People could learn a lot from wolves that way. Now this territory here, this was always taken care of by our family. No deeds to it, we just knew. It was a hundred years ago when the Stoners first got what they call legal title to this mountain. As if a man could own a mountain. Might as well lay claim to owning the air or the sunlight. The Stoners were stubborn, though, even though owning it was like carrying a weight heavy enough to crush you on your shoulders, like carrying a load of bad medicine. But we was stubborn, too. We kept on taking care of this land. . . the old way."

They stopped and Theo pointed with a stick. Louis bent close to look. He could see the steel trap there had the initials D.S. scratched onto it.

"Now it isn't right to take a man's traps, even when they're set where they shouldn't be. Even when that trapper's trying to catch so many game animals that he might end up wiping them out. But," Theo said, unbuttoning his fly, "there's nothing wrong with a wolf marking his territory in the old way. Sometimes I have to take along two extra canteens just to make it from one end of Old Stoner's trapline to the next."

Louis smiled again at the thought of that silent duel between the two old men, of all the years Old Stoner found empty traps still set and could not understand why the animals were avoiding them. Then he lifted his head to listen. From the other side of the hill he heard it again. The warning call of the bluejay, the guardian of the woods. Someone was coming along the trail. His heart beat faster in his chest and he felt the muscles between his shoulderblades tighten as he peered through the screen of branches which hid him from sight.

The tracks were almost too easy to follow. The paw marks of the wolf led right up the trail, marked deep in the soft earth by its edge. Danny-Boy knelt to look closer, wincing as he did from the pain in his ankle. It was certain sure that it was the same one he'd been following. There was one toe missing on the animal's right front track. Probably lost it in a steel trap. For a moment Danny-Boy wished he'd saved some of his old man's traps. Setting some of them up along these trails would be one way to make sure to get this damn animal. But after his father's death, his memories of the hours the old man made him spend cleaning and fixing those traps, had outweighed any urge he had to keep them. Instead he had loaded all of them into the back of a truck and taken them to the junk yard, a good half ton of iron.

Danny-Boy put his hand down and pressed it into the earth beside the wolf tracks. The paw marks were big, twice as big as those of a coyote, almost as big as a small bear.

"Bigger it is, easier it is to shoot," he said to himself. He wiped his hands on his shirt and stood up again. His ankle was stiff, but if he kept walking it would hold up. The tracks continued on over the hill, keeping to the left of the trail.

Someone came up the trail. The sunlight reflected off the rifle in his hands. There was dirt smudged across the man's face and a little blood on his right cheek, but Louis recognized the man. It was Danny-Boy Stoner. And as soon as he saw him, Louis knew why the man was there. Stoner was out to find the wolf and kill it. The sound of the trail bike must have been his and from the dirt on his face and his torn clothing, it was pretty clear that he'd dumped it somewhere back along the woods road.

For a moment Louis thought of standing, going down the slope to confront the man. But it was only a moment's impulse and he did not move. Something told him that Danny-Boy Stoner would shoot him as quick as he would a wolf. He watched as the big man knelt to look at something in the soft earth by the left side of the trail, wiped his hands on his shirt, and then rose and went on up the trail, around the bend and out of sight.

Louis counted slowly to a hundred. He made his way down to the trail. There were the marks of Stoner's boots, the indentation where he had pressed his left knee down, where he had leaned the butt of the gun down to help himself up as he stood. There, too, by the left side of the trail in a patch of soft earth bare of leaves was the clear imprint of the big man's left hand. But look as he might, Louis could find no other tracks and he found himself wondering. What was Stoner looking at?

Louis followed Stoner's tracks for half a mile, staying well back out of sight. He found two more spots where the big man had stopped again and knelt, put his hand down as if looking at something marked into the earth. But, as before, the only tracks were those of Stoner himself. Finally the trail came to the divide. The left branch swung down towards the beaver pond, one of the places where Danny-Boy's late father used to set traps. Down the hill was the way Danny-Boy's tracks went. Louis nodded. He wouldn't see the man again. He cut off from the trail and began to work his way up slope. Soon he found the trail Uncle Theo had marked. Not by piles of stones or by blazing trees, but in Theo's own way. There, along his special trail, every hundred paces was a tree branch in the shape of a circle. When those branches were thin and supple Theo had tied them that way. As they grew, they kept that shape. Louis rested his hand on one of those circled branches. The sun had been shining on it and it was warm to the touch. From far down the beaver valley behind him came the warning call of a bluejay, thin on the wind, marking Danny-Boy's downward progress.

The land rolled and folded like the covers of a bed after a fitful night. The trees were thick, the brush heavy. But as he followed Theo's trail, the way was easy. He felt as if he were no longer walking. Instead, the trail was opening under his feet and drawing him along. The sun was falling down the western slope of the sky as he glimpsed it now and then through the trees or around a brow of stone and he knew that he would have to spend the night at Theo's cabin when he came to it. He heard the trickle of water from over a small ridge. Theo's spring. He crested the ridge and looked down. It was there as he remembered it from his childhood. An old log lodge without windows. Even from only fifty yards away it was built so that it blended into the forest and was not easy to see. Its east-facing door was placed to be open to the morning sunlight slipping through the notch in the hills covered only by a thick hanging blanket. Louis remembered walking to that notch with Theo, seeing the sheer drop of cliff beyond it and understanding that only the sunlight could come to Theo's door from that direction.

As he walked towards the cabin he felt Uncle Theo was there. He looked into the door. It seemed as if he could see the shape of his uncle sitting in front of the stone hearth in the middle of the cabin. But the shape blurred into a ray of sunlight.

"Uncle Theo," he said. "I'm here."

A sort of vibration of light, the motion of a wind through the air of the old cabin, a feeling of warmth coming from inside. Nothing more than that, but also nothing less.

Louis looked behind the cabin. There in the woods, just as he had seen in his dream, were pens which had once been fenced in with strong wire mesh like dog runs. But the fences were broken down to set free the animals that had been kept there. There were many tracks around the cabin.

Louis walked to the top of the notch and sat with his feet dangling over the edge of the cliff. Almost dark. That time when you see the light that goes between the worlds. He slid the pack off his shoulders and took out the two cans of Dr. Pepper. He opened them both and poured one of them onto the stone of the cliff. He would not see Theo Lawless again in this lifetime. But his Uncle would always be with him.

Louis watched as evening spread over the land. There was nothing for him to fear in that darkness. A series of sounds echoed up from the long valley far below. The *BBBRRRAAATTT!* of an automatic rifle firing a single rapid burst. Then the sound of a man screaming in mortal fear, a scream cut short.

"You're right, Uncle Theo," Louis said to the night, "Our old people don't leave us."

How Mink Stole Time

Long ago, the People had no light. It was hard for them to move around in the darkness and they were always cold. Mink took pity on them. He heard that on the other side of the world there was something called the Sun. It was being kept there by those on the other side of the world. So Mink decided to steal the Sun for the People. It was not an easy job, but Mink was a great thief. He stole the Sun and placed it in the sky so that it would share its light equally with the people on both sides of the world. Now it was no longer dark and cold all the time. Now there was day and night because of the Sun.The People were very happy and they praised Mink. He grew proud of himself because of that praise.

"Perhaps," he said, "there is something else I can steal for the People."

A long time passed and Mink saw nothing that was worth stealing. Then the Europeans came. They were new people with a lot of power.

"What is it that these new people have that we do not have?" Mink said. Then he saw what it was. The Europeans had something they called Time. They used it to give them their power. So Mink decided he would steal Time. He waited until it was dark and sneaked into their house. There, in the biggest room, they kept Time up on a shelf. They kept it in a shiny box which made noises. As it made noises, two small arrows on the front of that box moved in circles. Mink could see it was a powerful thing. So he carried it off.

Now Mink and the People had Time. But Mink soon found that it was not easy to have Time. He had to watch the hands of that shiny box all of the time to see what the time was. He had to keep three keys tied around his neck so that he could use them to wind up that box full of time so it would keep on ticking. Now that Mink had Time, he no longer had the time to do the things he used to do. There was no time for him to fish and hunt as he had done before. He had to get up at a certain time and go to bed at a certain time. He had to go to meetings and work when that box full of time told him it was time. He and the People were no longer free.

Because Mink stole Time, it now owned him and the People. It has been that way ever since then. Time owns us the way we used to own the Sun.

The White Moose

His paddle moved in the quick shallow strokes used by the old Cree as he followed the edge of the long lake. His name French, his face showed another ancestry born to these northern forests. The lake was smooth as the panes of glass he'd seen in the windows of Quebec City. It reflected back the few clouds in the spring sky, the spruce trees along the shore. . . and a strange pale reflection which wavered as the ripple touched it, moving like fog pushed by the wind.

Jean Maurice moved his head slowly to find it in his peripheral vision. A moose calf of pure white. Next to it the big dark shape of the cow. He held the canoe with his paddle, turned the boat slowly. Move as the leaf moves touched by a wave. Now his eyes were directly on the two animals. To his surprise, both were looking straight at him. As if they had expected him to come.

He knew a man could come up on a moose from the water with relative ease, but to look it straight in the eyes this way? But it was so, he had heard, with albino animals. Along with their natural color, their fear was gone. As if protected by the young one's strange boldness, the cow moose stood there, too. Her jaws moved slowly, chewing the water plants she had just pulled from the lake. He was close enough to hear the sound of her eating, the drip of the water as it ran off her neck.

Then the calf looked away from him and began to nurse at its mother. The cow lifted her eyes past the man, as if seeing something behind him. The man looked back over his shoulder. All he saw was the other shore of the long lake.

He wrote the telegram a week later, wrote it at one of those moments when it seemed the quiet of his cabin and the empty chairs were too much for him to bear. He composed it slowly, letter by letter, for the Museum.

I find white moose. Calf still with mother. You want skin for mount?

His message went first to Quebec City. From there it made the longer, quicker journey to the heart of the continent. The head taxidermist read the letter. The man had collected for him in the past. Always sent them in good condition. Now the chance of a white moose calf. A good exhibit. But a full grown albino bull moose? The taxidermist smiled. No other museum in the world would have a full life mount of that! He composed his reply carefully.

Will pay top price for white moose if full grown bull. Inform when you have such. Do not collect until fully grown.

Like most of the hunters and trappers who lived off the north land — Indian and white alike — Jean Maurice knew more of the animals than did those far-away men who earned their living writing and teaching about them. Their studies meant only money, recognition and reputation. His studies, begun as a small child following his father's snowshoe tracks, meant life.

Jean Maurice's life was not easy, though once he would have chosen no other. He would not say that he *loved* the life he lived. Those who talked and wrote so much of *loving* the wilderness were not part of it. To speak of loving the woods would be like speaking of loving one's own self, for the woods were part of Jean Maurice — as much a part of him as the darkness of his eyes, the strength of his hands. And why should one talk of loving one's self, eh? So he might have said. But he was not a man who spoke much. Now, since the canoe tipped four springs ago, he spoke hardly at all.

The white calf stood, its head now reaching its tall mother's shoulder. Jean Maurice saw the cow's belly was swollen. Soon she would have the new calf. Eight moons since the time of fall rut when the mating calls of bulls trumpeted through the woods, the great horns clashed as they fought for the cows. This young white one had seen that, not far from the mother's side as she mated, returning to her when the rut was done, close by her side through the winter as she cleared away the snow for him to graze, kept the wolves from him. Soon, though, it would be the time for the new one to come. Then the mother would drive away this strange calf whose color was that of the winter.

Jean Maurice knew the calving time, when the cows go to the willow thickets to bear their young. It was also the fattening time for the packs of wolves. They followed the moose, waiting for the weak animal, the exhausted one, the one crippled by disease. The wolves never took the most healthy.

Like their brother Wolf, Jean Maurice's old people took only certain ones. In the summer, they would kill a strong young cow with no calf, knowing she was barren, had not continued the cycle. That was the right way. They knew which animal they would kill. The men in the cities wrote about the Cree. *The lives of these woodland hunters are full of uncertainty. They may not find game. It is feast one week and famine the next.*

"Tomorrow," Jean Maurice's uncle would say, "we are going to kill that female moose between the forked lake and the grey peak. We will take it when the sun is four hands above the western edge of the world."

Jean Maurice tried once to explain it to a city man for whom he guided. For the Cree, it was as it was for the city people going to a store. Just as the city people knew what food was in the stores, so the Cree knew what was in the forests. Their hunting skills were like the money the city people used to buy things. And what of the uncertainties, the dangers of life in the wilderness? Ah, was that not there in the cities also? Jean Maurice had seen how quickly the motor cars traveled in Quebec City. They were dangerous and sometimes killed people. Were there not more of them in Chicago? Was that not the place where — he had heard, though being only an ignorant man he could not say if it were true — there were many men with guns like those used in the Great War? Men killing each other in the streets because of the gambling and the illegal liquor? How could one survive in such a dangerous place? In the woods, one knew what dangers existed, that storms might come, that a dead tree might fall in a high wind (and so one never camped near a dead tree), that a canoe might overturn. The man had been unconvinced. The next spring Jean Maurice's own canoe, carrying his wife and child, had overturned.

The letter from the Field Museum folded at the bottom of his pack, Jean Maurice followed the cow and white one through the second year. The time of calving was close. Many cows were in the willow thickets, heavy with their time. The young which would weigh no more than his pack, yet wobble to their feet ready to run as soon as their mothers licked free the birth sack. From time to time he saw the tracks of wolves. He remembered the story his grandfather told.

Long ago, the old man said, the wolves discovered that the moose were easy prey when they gave birth. The packs would follow a cow till her time came and then take both the mother and young. There was little risk then from the cow's hooves which could cripple or kill.

The Keeper of the Game saw that it was not right. The Keeper of the Game was not an animal, though it appeared in that form, white as the winter snows. It was a spirit, part of the Great Manitou, a powerful being showing itself in animal shape. It called together the moose.

"Children," said the Keeper of the Game, "I have seen how hard it is with you now. I want you and your children and the children of your children to survive on this earth. When you give birth to your young, then for a time you are weak and helpless. That is when the wolves, as is their right, come to prey upon you. I cannot chase away the wolves. It is good that they should take the weak and the sick. Those who survive will be stronger. There will be less disease. Now, however, it is too easy for the wolves. Thus, things must change now. Now it will be as I say. During the moon when the buds swell, when the snow moves back and the marshes sing, then the cows with young will all go to the willow thickets. All will give birth then, within the space of the rising and setting of a few suns. So many of you will be helpless, so many of you weak, they cannot prey upon you all. They will take the weakest first. Then, when they have killed and eaten, they will be full and lazy and will not hunt again for a time. In that time you will regain strength. Your young will learn to run. Then both moose and wolf will continue and the balance will be right."

The pregnant calf and her white yearling went into the willow thickets and Jean Maurice followed. He watched her give birth to twin calves. The wolves came and took the smaller of the two before the mother could drive them away. The wolves stalked stiff-legged around the white yearling, neither touching or looking at it. The white moose made no attempt to run from those who carry death in their eyes, those wolf eyes which, when you are an animal who has given yourself to them, become strangely soft and clear.

Jean Maurice had seen it, that moment between the wolves and their prey when something seemed to pass between their eyes. Then a sort of agreement was reached, the chase was ended. He remembered the old elk, its one eye clouded and blind. It stood calmly, not running like the others. The wolves, too, stopped running. The elk lowered its head until its nose almost touched that of the big grey wolf which came up to it — almost like a dog coming up to its master, tail held up. They stood there for a moment, their eyes locked. Then the elk was dragged down, the pack pulling at it.

In the days when Jean Maurice wandered the woods after the accident, he thought that would not be a bad way to die. Better than choking on the cold waters. He saw the heads of his wife and son go under. He wondered why he had been swept up to shore, why there had been strength enough in his limbs to pull himself from that glacier-cold embrace of water where no human can live more than a few heartbeats. He wondered why the sun struck so warmly on that bank, melting the snow from his veins. He wondered why he lived and not those two he found further down the stream. There he buried them, piling many stones high in a cairn to keep out the carcajou, leaving his tobacco pouch hung from a stick wedged between the stones. One day, Jean Maurice decided, he would die like the elk. He would not seek death, but when it came, he would look into the fierce kindness of its eyes.

Yet the wolves avoided the eyes of the white moose, even as it seemed to ignore them. He wondered if it was like the other albino animal he had seen, a scrawny raccoon with pink, almost sightless eyes which he found dead at the base of a tree. But no, the white moose was not like that. Its eyes were dark. It could see and hear as well as any animal. Yet it seemed to feel no threat from anything. It was as if it were immune to the ways of the natural world which other animals must live by — immune to those ways or above them.

In the fall, another message came. The man at the Field Museum had changed his mind. He was worried about the trophy escaping. The paper read:

Take white moose now, if possible.

Jean Maurice read the message again and placed it in the small fire in front of him. He could see, in the valley below, the paleness of the young bull, its first rack of horns now losing their velvet skin coating. It waded in the beaver meadow, dipping its head deep under the water to graze on the lilies and arrowroot. He had sent his message back to Chicago:

Cannot find now.

"You grow first," Jean Maurice said. Then, putting out his fire, he walked down the back of the ridge through the pines.

Four years passed. Each fall messages came from the man at the Field Museum. Once a man was sent from Chicago to help find the white moose. Jean Maurice led them far to the west of the place where the white one grazed. He had made his promise to take the white one when it was well grown. He would keep that promise. But he would help no one else to do so and he would not do it himself before the time was right. The man from Chicago went back to the museum with many dark-furred trophies and the promise that Jean Maurice would collect the moose, the white moose, whenever it was possible.

Four years. It was the time when the red of the Great Bear's blood came down from the sky where the Sky Hunters killed it each autumn. The leaves of the trees were scarlet from the blood of the Great Bear. The velvet was gone from the antlers of the bull moose and the willow thickets and spruce patches were marked by their horns and hooves. Jean Maurice went carefully through the woods, skirting the clearings where bulls had pawed the ground, marking it with their urine to lure the cows. He saw, too, the tracks of the wolf packs. They were gathering to take the most exhausted of the bulls. Bodies steaming with sweat, legs shaking from the exertion of battling, some with great wounds on their bodies from the prongs and hooves of stronger bulls, they would become prey to the wolves. It would be a quicker and kinder death than the slow weakness into the winter season, stores of fat depleted by their fighting, their wounds festering. All around the fighting grounds small trees were broken, brush flattened by the plunging and clashing of great animals, each seven feet tall at the shoulder and weighing more than half a ton. Throughout the wilds the striking together of their massive racks was the beat of an ancient music, a song of continuing their blood lines. When the season of rut ended there would be fewer bulls. After the winter there would be no more than one bull for every two cows, the mothers-to-be coming into the new year, the promise of the future in their wombs, the balance right, the cycle continuing.

Jean Maurice pulled the canoe out of the place it was hidden in the alders. He stepped in and pushed off from shore with a quick motion. He held in one hand the calling horn of birch bark. He could go, he knew, to the place where the white one could be found, but this was the way to do it. If it came, he would know the time was right.

He let the canoe float for a time, feeling the dead calm of the air around him. The wind, before it died, had been in his face. He looked towards the shore, lifted the birch bark cone to his lips and began, softly at first.

"*Moo–wauh–yuh,*" he called, imitating the voice of a cow seeking a mate. "*Moo–wauh–yuh.*" He called for a long time, louder each time until the still air above the small lake was filled with that sound. "*MOO–WAUH–YUH.*"

It would be coming now, coming from two valleys away, coming to this small lake where he had watched it dip its head to graze the waterweeds. The day's light was thinning. He paused and listened. Something was close to the edge of the lake. The brush parted and the white moose stood there. It looked into his eyes as it had that first day. A bird was riding on its left shoulder. The beard of the white moose, was long and full below its chin. The span of its horns were as wide and well-balanced as any he had ever seen.

Jean Maurice raised his gun.

"I do as I promised," he said.

The specimen arrived at the Field Museum in perfect condition. He was more than pleased. For some time now he'd felt uncertain about the man. Now he told his secretary to go ahead and fill out the request for the funds to be wired to Quebec City.

He spread the skin out on the table. The half-breed had done his job well, skinning it out cleanly, salting it down. HANDLE WITH CARE had been marked on the box and it had been handled with care along the way, despite the accidents. The boat which carried it down the river sank, though the box washed up onto shore. The train which carried it had experienced first a fire and then a derailment. The truck which brought it from the train station had been involved in a collision on its way across town to the museum.

Now, though, it was here. Perfect for a fullsize life mount. It would be, he saw, gigantic. One of the biggest ever seen. He had a form prepared, but it was clear he'd have to build up the shoulders, thicken the neck. He picked up a knife, began to trim away a few pieces of loose flesh at the edge of the skin. Then, as if it had a mind of its own, the knife jumped in his hand. He grabbed at it, dropped it.

"Hell!" he said. He was bleeding. A little cut. But the bleeding wouldn't stop. Pulsing from his hand. He wrapped his handkerchief, saw it turn crimson. Pressed harder on his wrist. Walked towards the door, light-headed now, a roaring noise in his ears.

"Miss Keely, I need help!" No answer from the other side of that door — paler now, further away.

"White animals," the Director said, "are invested with all sorts of special significance by superstitious peoples. Associated, perhaps, with the threatening powers of the winter. Perhaps a racial memory of the glacial periods. Some even say, you know, that the white is associated in primitive minds with a kind of purity. Interesting superstitions."

"Like the Virgin Mary in your Catholic stories?" said his visitor.

"Oh?" The Director said. He continued down the hall, followed by the slender man with dark hair. "But this is the room where it's being prepared. You'll see what I mean."

He opened the door. In the preparation room a man and woman were working on a huge animal, so white as to appear made out of snow. They were combing down the fur, painting around the nostrils, tying string to the ears so they would dry in place, putting the final touches on the mount.

"The Wilsons," the Director said. "Brought them in, as you may have heard, after Conroy. Poor man. First cut himself and almost bled to death, then didn't know the hand was infected. Must have been from the knife. Wouldn't come back after that, even though it was his baby. Fortunate the Wilsons were available." He smiled at the man and woman who nodded and smiled back. Above them, the white moose's head was lifted as if listening to something very far away. Its eyes were dark and shining.

"So, Mr. Prey," the Director said, "with your own Indian background, Ottawa isn't it? Think you can paint us a fitting background for this Great White Spirit Animal of ours?" There was no answer. The Director turned around in time to see the man's hand vanishing as he closed the door behind him.

The Wilsons finished their work late in the day. The Director walked with them to the door and shook hands before starting down the street.

"Damn strange," the Director said to himself. "I thought he wanted work." He watched as the two taxidermists walked along the avenue. Then he opened his mouth to shout. By the time the noise came from his throat, it was only a small strangled cry. The cornice which came loose from the new building had already struck. The Director ran across the street, his chest tight, holding his breath. He let it out as he saw it had not fallen on them, just near them. They were leaning against the building. Alive. But the bricks struck with such force that they exploded like shrapnel. Wilson held up his wife in the crook of his arm and the Director could see that both of them were bleeding from deep wounds in their hands.

The exhibit finally opened. But it didn't have the popularity the museum had expected. People seemed uninterested... uncomfortable with it. Children would not stay in the room. The big animal was watching them. Some said they saw it moving. When the fire struck the exhibit hall it was with a sense of relief that the Director looked at the ruins of the room and saw the white moose lying on its side, blackened from the smoke.

"No, we won't try to restore it."

Spring came again to the northern woods. Jean Maurice paddled his canoe along a way he had followed many times before. It had not been a good winter. Once again he had lost a canoe. With it went all of a winter's catch of furs and the gun. He hadn't been in the boat. It had broken free from the bank as if with a life of its own. His good skinning knife had broken, fire had gutted his cabin.

Within himself, he knew. Because of the white one. Yet why had nothing happened to him physically? Why were only his *things* taken? Because I lost myself already. He thought of that for many days. There were no more accidents.

It would have been easy to replace his things with the money from the museum. The check was a big one. He gave it to the small

Catholic church in the town at the edge of the forest. No more museums.

He dipped his paddle into the silent water, gliding the edge of the lake towards a pale reflection. He looked. There on the bank was a cow moose and a white calf. Its incredible eyes looked into his, its gaze unconcerned and knowing.

Jean Maurice smiled. "Live long, Little Brother," he said. Then, his heart feeling strong and good, he paddled around the bend.

The Trout

They had been fishing all day. Luck was bad. They headed back, poles over their shoulders, kicking at leaves.

–Hey, you hear something?

–Maybe.

–Seems to be coming from that tree there.

–There's a hollow halfway up, might be a bear.

–I'm going to check it out.

He climbs, climbs, climbs until his friend on the ground thinks he is going to climb into the clouds.

–I didn't think this tree was so tall. Say, you ought to see this!

–I'm not climbing up there.

–This is really something.

–What is it?

–You would *not* believe it.

–Tell me.

His head and shoulders are inside the hollow in the tree. His voice echoes out, deep as thunder or a giant's drum.

–There is a pool of water in here. A trout is swimming around in it, a big pretty trout. I'm going to catch it.

–You better leave it alone.

–No, I've almost . . . I've got it!

He comes down the tree. The trout is flopping in his hands.

–This is really a beauty.

–Put it back.

–Why should I?

He kills the trout and cleans it, throwing the guts into the underbrush.

–Hey, I'm hungry. Let's eat it right here.

–I don't want any.

He builds a fire from the dead lower branches of the hollow tree and begins to cook the trout.

–Boy, does this smell good! You sure you don't want any?

–I'm sure.

He starts to eat the fish, eating faster and faster until he has eaten it all, even the bones.

–Now I feel thirsty.

–There's a spring back there.

–Good, I'm going to get a drink. I'll be right back.

The friend sits by the hollow tree. He waits for a long time and then goes to look for him. He finds him kneeling by the stream, his face thrust into the water.

–Haven't you had enough to drink?

–No, I'm still thirsty.

–What did you say? Your voice is funny.

He looks up from his drinking. His lips are round and large, shaped like the lips of a fish.

–I'm still thirsty.

He bends his head and starts drinking again. The friend stays with him until it is dark.

–I have to go.

–That's all right. I will stay here.

His whole face has changed now. His head looks like the head of a fish. The friend goes home. When he comes back the next day the spring has widened and deepened into a pond. He doesn't see the man anywhere.

–I'm here.

–Where?

–Down here.

He looks into the water at the big fish which has just come to the surface.

–Here I am. Now listen to me! Tell all the people they can catch many fish in this pond. But tell them they have to do it right. When they catch a fish they have to say a thanksgiving to it, they have to put the parts they don't eat where the animals of the forest can come and share them. They have to only catch as many fish as they need, no more. You listen to me and tell them. You were right. I'm sorry I didn't listen to you. Speak to my family for me. The people can always catch many fish here if they do it right. Goodbye.

–from a Seneca story

Notes From a Morning of Fishing

A canvas creel, hip boots that belonged to my father, a green belt-loop container for worms, a Swiss Army knife purchased in Lugano and tied to my belt by a length of rawhide, an elastic band to secure my glasses against the slide of sweat and the tug of small fingers of twigs, a bottle of Cutter's lotion, a collapsible fiberglass fly rod — each item taken from the place it was kept, part of the quiet routine of getting ready, preparing my mind as well, assembling scattered pieces which, when fit together, become a map.

I begin by fishing under bridges, places passed over by a thousand cars every day. After a heavy rain, trout run upstream and hole up in such places, ecological niches waiting to be filled. The place where you catch a trout one week will hold another the next.

My line drifts into the culvert then snaps tight. I set the hook and reel in a ten inch brook trout. Wood ducks are talking in the marsh behind us as I pin the fish down, grasp its body. There's a ritual I always follow, one I've taught my sons. We are connected to the lives around us, to this one life I am about to take. "Thank you for letting me catch you," I say. Then, my thumb inside its mouth, my index finger on its spine, I break the trout's neck. Its teeth make small red scratches on the knuckle of my thumb. The Inuit people melt a handful of snow in their mouths and then let it fall into the mouth of each seal they harpoon. "Here is the water you were thirsty for," they say. They know that the seals will not allow themselves to be caught if they are not given a drink of fresh water.

Taking out my knife, I insert it into the ventral opening of the fish to slit its stomach. The sharp blade slides smoothly as a zipper and the intestines bulge out. The full stomach, cut by the blade, disgorges a four inch minnow, shiny as cellophane. I drop the minnow into the stream, which is named Dunham Brook, named after my great-grandfather's people. The sticky fluid from the fish makes a filmy rainbow between my hand and the knife. I make a second cut behind the neck of the trout and the head comes free, still attached to the guts. I clean the knife on the grass, wipe it on my leg, fold it and put it back into my pocket. "Thank you," I say again. Then I throw the head and guts into the swamp. Other fish, a raccoon, the flies — something will take it. Give back what you cannot use. I drop the trout into the canvas creel and wash my hands in startlingly cold water.

As I walk in half a mile from Bockes Road to find the small, unnamed stream which flows into Kayaderosseras Creek, I see how things remain the same yet change each year along these banks. Here and there the familiar path is blocked by trees knocked down in the big wind of late winter. There is a small waterfall which can be heard as you push through the underbrush, out of sight of the stream which is buried in raspberry tangles. I use that sound as a mariner uses a compass, navigating my way back to the place where I pulled out a 16 inch long brown trout a year ago. The singing of the falls grows louder and then I step out of brush and almost into water. Kneeling, I play out line. A ripple on the surface, a small tug, then the line dives down and it tangles in the slats of a wooden barrel this year's spring freshet brought downstream. The fish slips free and the line is left in a knot around the mossy planks. I wade in and untangle it. Another day and I'll try for this trout again.

Some places along the Kayaderosseras, where there are deep pools not far from the road, the fish are skittish from too many heavy-footed fishermen, ignoring even the most carefully placed lures. Here, though, I find as much pleasure in crawling up through the grasses and the summer blossoms of daisy and scarlet stream's edge Cardinal flower, to lean out inch by inch and see them just below me, almost close enough to touch. My fingers grasp the stones and I hover above the water as the trout hover within the current. They are motionless except for the small shiver of their fins, facing into the current, waiting for whatever the flow will bring them. At moments like this, trout in a stream are like sunlight — flickering, bright, quick, vanishing with the first cloud.

A hurricane wind came through this grove of tall white pines by the edge of the creek almost five years ago. The big trees which were uprooted then have grown smaller since their fall. Limbs have rotted away in the moist woods and the massive trunks have settled further each year into the soil. Climbing over them, I see the bone yellow wood flake away beneath my fingers. The scent of pine stays on my hands and there are bits of crumbled wood tissue under my fingernails. Crawling over the last of the toppled giants, I have reached the junction of the Kayaderosseras and the little feeder brook. A trout whips out of the ripple before I can drop in my line, escaping into the deeper water of the Kayaderosseras.

Instead of following the stream I climb over a hill. It is an esker. An old Irish word meaning a ridge, an esker is a long narrow shape of coarse gravel deposited by a stream flowing in the ice-walled valley in a decaying glacial ice sheet. It is covered now by a soft blanket of several millennia of pine needles and leafmold, but it reminds me of the strength of those forces which have shaped this earth, the tenuousness of our own tenancy of these hills. Coming down its other side, I am in another world. Here the pines have been replaced by hemlocks. Their trunks almost purple, their roots have grown into the stream or been exposed by its serpentine turnings through the forest. In places there are holes as much as seven feet deep diving back in an equal distance beneath the shallow umbrella-rooted hemlocks. Sometimes lunker trout lurk in those dark shelters. Two days ago heavy rain made the water rise, washing over the banks. It is down now, but the grasses and flowers along the stream are still slicked down and just starting to stand — like the protesting cowlick of a boy. Floating my worm into one hole after another I catch a fish each time. None are more than ten inches long and the smallest ones, lightly held by the barbless hook, I return to the water.

The roots of the trees which move like the tentacles of sea anemones in the current are bright, almost glowing. For some reason they are many different colors: cimarron red, cobalt blue, lemon yellow, housepaint white and sienna brown. When I lift their tips from the water the color seems to fade and almost vanish. I step across the stream at its narrowest point and my eyes suddenly focus on the stub of a hemlock branch right in front of my nose. A slug is perched there, two inches long, yellow as a banana. It has eight black spots on its side as if, like the banana it reminds me of, it is ripening. It is as unmoving as the branch itself. *Hello.*

After coming back out to the car, I drive down Dunham Pond Road, stopping where a small and slightly stagnant creek, fed by the spring in the midst of Arnold's cow pasture, leads into marsh. There is something brown moving in the water. It is a muskrat, long tail oaring him along. He tries to dive and escape my gaze, but the water isn't deep enough. He doesn't seem to be that afraid, though, and my laughter doesn't seem to bother him much. Finally he just climbs out on the bank and sits quietly under some wild grapevines, a bunch of dark purple fruit bobbing near his head. He watches me as I watch him.

A bit further down the road in that same marsh someone's minnow trap floats behind an alder. *Thunnk!* There is a strange call, like the sound of a stake being driven into the ground. Wings flap a few yards back in behind the sedge. I wait and the call is repeated. *Thunnk!* Then a heron lifts up out of the water, flies a few feet and perches in the top of a small maple which was drowned when the waters rose after the beavers built their dam downstream three springs ago. The heron arches its neck and calls again. *Thunnk!*

Bell Brook is the stream right behind our house. It is the place where I begin and end, the first stream I fished as a boy, the first stream where my older son caught a fish. Today I stop where its headwaters come close to the road a ways north of our home. A year ago, when the stream dried up two miles south of here as it does each year — the slower waters going down below the bedrock to a subterranean stream that emerges again a mile further down before it, too, joins the Kayaderosseras by way of Putnam Brook — I found more than a dozen trout cut off in a pool rapidly losing oxygen as it warmed. I put them into a bucket and took them to this place where the stream seems too shallow to hold a trout. Here, though, the flow is cold and sweet and deeper than it seems, sometimes going down four feet and more below the false bottom formed by the thick growth of watercress, duckweed and other aquatic plants. Beavers have moved in here, too, this year. Their dam is too close to the source and I walk out onto it and pry free a few branches, press with a foot on the mud-packed surface until water washes through. Downstream the water is needed. I know that by tomorrow morning the dam will be repaired once more, but in this small matter I assert my human right to interfere.

At times it seems as if beavers are like the Army Corps of Engineers. I recall a cartoon in one of the wildlife conservation texts I studied at Cornell. It showed a crazy-eyed man in a hardhat with a steamshovel behind him and the name ARMY CORPS OF ENGINEERS on its side. They were chasing one tiny raincloud across a parched landscape. "Quick," the caption read, "there's a drop of water!" But beavers differ greatly from the Army Corps. For one, they don't have a particular fondness for building on Indian reservations, inundating large segments of what little land is left to Native Americans. The beaver and the Native American always co-existed in good balance. In fact, this balance lasted until European demands for beaver hats led to the extermination of the beaver in the east and the great fur-trapping wars between Indian nations which hastened the divide and conquer success of the whites in the struggle for North America. Indian people like the beaver. They hunted beaver, ate them and used their pelts, but they also made a practice of bringing young beavers into their homes. It was even common for Iroquois women with small babies to nurse an orphaned beaver kit at their other breast. Native Americans admired the beaver for their industriousness. They were right to do so. Much of the good meadowland of North America is the result of old beaver ponds which filled in with rich silt, grew tall grass. Where beavers went the fish and the birds, the moose and the deer would follow. The face of this land was changed as much by the beavers as by the force of the glaciers.

From my morning of fishing I bring home six trout which we will eat for dinner. And I bring home more than that, things which would have been enough even if I had caught no fish at all. I think of the bear hunt my father went on years ago. He saw plenty of bears, but he didn't fire a shot. "He counted coup with his eyes," my Cheyenne friend, Lance Henson, said when I told him about it. Each autumn my father shot a deer and its meat lasted us through much of the winter. But he had no wish, no need, to shoot a bear. Just to look at one now and then.

To go through life as a fish goes through water, leaving little or nothing changed by your passing — or perhaps to go as a beaver does, making dams which may be in the wrong place now and then but which more often than not leave things changed in a way which is part of the flow, good for the earth and for generations to come — this morning of fishing reminds me that is what I want to do.

Bears

I

Somebody asked me once why we Indians are so funny about bears, how come we think they are so special. I didn't know quite how to answer that question then. I just grunted and kept working on fletching an arrow. And it wouldn't have been polite to ask why white people *don't* think bears are special.

I've done some thinking about it since. A bear is a lot like a person. Or maybe it's the other way around, seeing as how the stories tell us that some of us are descended from bears. You take the skin off a bear, it looks pretty much like a human being and according to one of the tales that was what bears used to be able to do on their own. They could take their skins off, put on human clothes and then act just like a regular human being — except maybe a little more polite. They'd usually do it because they had the hots for some village maiden they'd seen out berry-picking and they wanted to marry her. And then there are the stories — not so old, now — about the bearmen, the medicine men who can put on a bear skin and then turn into a bear, walk like a bear. They have a lot of power like that, but if you're brave enough to wait up at night and hide near the place where one of those bearwalkers is going and then jump out and grab them, they have to give you all you want. Money, power, you name it. Problem is, you got to make sure it is a bearwalker and not a real bear. You grab a real bear when it is walking at night and it will give you all you want — but it won't be money or power. Grab and take your chance.

There's only one road through Sullivan Park, even though you might think there were more from the way it circles and dips around and over the two big hills. The road begins at a pair of stone gates — like those of a prison or an exclusive school. You pass through them and find yourself rising up that first hill that seems to end at the top, going right up into the sky. But when you reach that crest you come down fast and the first thing you see — or smell — is the duck pond of the zoo.

Its stagnant water fills the night, even a clear autumn one like this. I could smell that there would be rime on the grass at dawn, that the scummy surface of the small fenced-in pond would be white with ice, patterns as delicate as those of a bird's feathers brushed across its surface by Hatho, the frost spirit. One of the few places in the city limits where there still was an expanse of water for him to work his old magic. Like most Indians today he has had to adapt to new times, do his artwork on windows as ponds and streams become less frequent. But at Swenoga he still walks through the woods on winter days. You may not see him, but if you walk back in a ways you'll hear him on a cold day, striking the trees with his stone ax, making them crack in the old way.

As I sat next to Peter in the front seat of his red van I thought about grabbing a bear and about what we were about to try to do. Try to do. Neither of us were talking, but I could still hear his voice as he told me about the bear while we sat in my lodge. Then, the rain falling, the familiar bark walls around us, it all seemed so logical.

"It's dying, Foxy. Or it's going to die if it stays there. It just walks back and forth, back and forth in that cage. It doesn't look like it is looking at anything. But when it stops you can see that its eyes are always looking towards the hills. Towards Swenoga. I've watched it so often that I feel like I'm in that cage with it. I can see it when I dream. I keep dreaming about it. Nights the kids from the projects climb over the fences and get into the zoo. I've seen what they do. They vandalize the place, spray paint their names, kill the ducks — knock their heads off with grass whips — and they do things to the animals in open cages — like the bear. I spent a long time looking in that bear's eyes, Foxy, and I swear it was trying to tell me something. It just stopped and looked at me for a long time. Stopped pacing back and forth and looked at me. And as soon as I started thinking there was nothing I could do to help it started moaning and pacing again. So I decided to do something and I decided to ask if you could help me. You know why I want you to help me."

Yup, I knew why. It was because of all the stories I'd told him about bears. But now it wasn't a story. It was very late at night and we were heading for the zoo in a panel truck planning to liberate a bear. I sighed and shook my head. How did I get into this? Well, I'd agreed to come along and I was stuck with it. But at least I knew Peter had to have a good plan. Lawyers always have good plans. He probably had a tranquilizer gun or nets in the back of the van and knew exactly what he was going to do.

Peter heard my sigh and looked over at me, my face illuminated for a moment by the stop light on Sullivan Boulevard. Pretty soon we'd reach that statue of that old Indian fighter, heroic burner of cornfields and girdler of fruit trees.

"I know," Peter said, "it makes me sigh, too, whenever I think about that zoo."

"Hmmm," I said. What else could I say? We rode along in silence a while longer as the streets grew darker. We were getting close to Sullivan Park. I wondered what sort of plan Peter *did* have.

"Foxy?"

"Yep?"

"How the hell are we going to do this?"

I closed my eyes and put my hand over my mouth like I was thinking. Actually I was holding my mouth shut to keep it from saying *Let Me Out Of Here!* I thought, too, about accidentally leaning too hard against the door handle so the door would swing open and I'd fall out. We weren't going too fast, but if I was lucky I'd end up with a couple of broken bones. That'd be better than ending up in jail. But I didn't do it. I knew why. Peter was right. Now that we had said it, now that we had realized it, that bear was like our brother. It was like an Indian. It was a part of Creation as much as we were and we'd promised to do something and now we had to do it. Something.

During the war I saw that sometimes the best plan is to have no plan at all. There was one general who made it all the way across North Africa, confusing the hell out of Rommell, by never having a plan. That general was always making mistakes, too. He'd take a wrong turn and attack at places no sane man would dream of attacking. The Germans always figured he had some master plan they couldn't understand and so they would retreat or get so confused they would make even bigger mistakes themselves and then lose. Sometimes you just have to get into things and then work it out from there. And I was in it now.

"Peter," I said, "that road there goes to the Sphinx Mall, don't it?"

Ten minutes later I came out of the Fatz Stationery Store with a bundle under my arm. We'd made it just five minutes before closing time. I opened the door of the van with my left hand and heaved the bundle up on the seat in front of me.

"Stencils and fast-drying spray paint," I said. "I ever tell you about the time I worked as a sign painter, Peter?"

Half an hour later a van pulls through the gates of the Zoo, allowed in by a bored night watchman who pays little attention to it, or to its driver (long hair stuffed under a cap), or to the fact that the letters that spelled out ATTICA UNIVERSITY ZOOLOGY DEPARTMENT waver a bit out of a straight line.

Sullivan Park is not quiet at night. It might seem that way to someone who doesn't listen or know how to listen, but not to me. There's a small wind in the trees, but that isn't the sound I'm hearing. Animals make noises at night. In the woods those noises are natural. Here they aren't. They're like the sounds children make when they are about to drift off into a sleep that they know is going to be full of nightmares. Bad dreams of teenage kids carrying long sticks with razor blades embedded in the end. Just long enough to reach into cages. Long enough to slash the heads off the ducks or geese unwary enough to bed down near the edge of their pond where they are still within reach. Whimpering sounds. Sounds that will make me dream bad when I remember them in years to come. Nightmares, but nightmares acted out by kids whose own lives are too often like nightmares when they are awake. The kids like those found O.D.ed on cocaine or black heroin. They found two of them last week near the west fence to the park. Now the guards watch the fences more carefully. Let them die in their own neighborhoods but not here. Here only animals are supposed to be dying.

I shake my head. This place fills my head with the wrong kind of thoughts.

"You think we should wait a little, Foxy?" Peter says.

"Drive around a little more."

Peter glances at his watch. 10:30 P.M.

"You think we ought to do it now, Foxy?"

This time when he asks me I groan. It is the fourth time he has asked, looking at his watch each time. The second time he asked I asked him what he had in the back to keep the bear under control. You need something, he said? I didn't answer him. It is my own damn fault for letting him think I can talk to animals. Well, I can talk to animals. But that doesn't mean they are going to listen to me. The third time he asked I just grunted and shook my head. Part of me was hoping that a night watchman would wonder why we were parked in front of the empty administration building. That same part of me that was weighing whether it was better to go to jail for unsuccessfully attempting to get a bear out of its cage or to end up in the hospital after getting it out successfully and finding myself between it and freedom. Talk to animals. What do you say to a four hundred pound black bear? It is like what you say to a four hundred pound gorilla. You say 'Sir!'

So when Peter asks me I groan. Oh my oh my, a little moan escaping my lips. Oh oh oh oh. But as I moan I see Peter starting to tap his hand on the wheel. Somehow my moaning is coming out like a song. I moan a little louder and by gosh I am singing. Somehow. It doesn't even sound too bad and as I listen to my own voice I begin to feel better. An old Swenoga social dance song. A Bear dance, by gosh!

When I've finished the song I feel real good. "What time is it, Peter?"

"Midnight."

"Okay. It's time."

Bears are funny animals. Like people. You never know what to expect from a bear. That's like people, too. Friend of mine, Choctaw guy, traveled for years with the circus and he learned what the most dangerous job was. Not the Lion Tamer or the tightrope walker. Nope, the Bear Trainer. Working with those big, clumsy-looking loveable Russian Brown Bears. Like big teddy bears wearing funny hats and riding bicycles. But you never knew what they were thinking, my Choctaw friend said. You could tell when another animal was getting bad, but a bear might be good one minute and bad the next. Moody. Like to do things their own way. Carry grudges, he said. He'd feed 'em but he was damned if he was ever going to be talked into working with them in the shows. Saw one big Russian Brown swipe the face right off his trainer then get back on his little bicycle and pedal around the ring while they were looking for a gun or a net and carrying the trainer off. After hundreds of years of being trained, being clowns and captives and star attractions in little shows all over the world, deep down inside bears have never accepted that as their place, never accepted belonging to anyone but themselves and the Creator. Like Indian people. And if you think you own a bear, then don't expect it to be your friend.

We're parked right behind the hill against which the bear cages are placed. Right next to the cage where the one remaining black bear is kept. There's a tree stump next to us. As I get out of Peter's truck I place my hand on top of that stump. The tree has been cut down only a few days before and little ridges of ice have formed from the bleeding rings. I think of what each of those rings means, each one a full cycle of the seasons. Together they span all the generations since the white people claimed this part of the continent. It was an old tree, though not as old as some. But still old enough to have been here longer than any single human life. The rings are thinner on this stump near the outside, thinner as they came closer to the present. Tree rings are not all the same thickness. In good years, years good for trees and other living things, the rings are thick. Peter is looking at me in the half-darkness created by the light diffused through the bars from a carbon arc streetlamp fifty yards away.

"This one," I say, "lived a long time. Back when it was young our people used its bark to make longhouses, canoes, bowls. They burned its wood for their cooking fires. I know people say now that elm don't burn good. It's tough wood, all right, tough to split, hard to cut. But we used it and we didn't complain. Wherever there were elm trees, we were there, too. Then they came. They brought the disease with them. The trees got sick, their tops died away first, their branches began to fall. Like this tree, they died. All the elm trees are dying. You know, Peter, when all the elms are finally dead, I want to be dead."

Peter reaches out and puts his hand on the stump next to mine. The ice is melting from the warmth of our hands. "Do you feel it?" he says.

"What?" I say, but I think I already know.

"Like somebody — or something — is watching us."

"Yes," I say.

"I think what we are going to do is right," he says.

I stand there, feeling that the life isn't all gone out of that elm tree, feeling as if its sap is flowing up through my fingers into my arms. I'm thinking the words of the old thanksgiving speech, the one my people always used to say at the start of any ceremony, any great undertaking.

I find myself remembering all the living things, greeting them and thanking them. The earth, the trees, the running streams, all those things which give us life. Then I am no longer just thinking them, I am saying them and Peter is speaking with me. Our voices aren't loud, but I can feel everything around us that is not human has begun to listen. Listen. Listen. When I finish and take my hand away from the stump it seems as if the air is clean around us. I feel young and strong. And I'm thinking that getting a bear out of a locked cage is no big thing to do at all. Just bend open the bars and carry it away like you'd pick up a puppy. But that strong feeling only lasts a moment and I can feel myself growing weak and small and old again. But this time it is different. I may be weak and small and old, but I'm not alone.

"What's that little building over there?" I say. There's a small shed that is painted a dark color, so dark we hadn't seen it before, even though it is less than thirty feet away. Its door is held closed by a sliding bolt. Unlocked. I slide it back, swing open the door. Peter flicks his pocket lighter and we both smile at what I pick up from the floor. I hand it to Peter.

"Ever use a bolt cutter before?"

I close the door to the shed, feeling once again the presence of approving watchers.

"If things keep going this way," I say, "I'm going to start saving my fingernails again for you people."

"Who?" Peter says. "Fingernails."

"I'll explain it later." We've reached the walkway in front of the cages and I'm looking around.

"Entrance door's back there."

"Just lookin'," I say. A row of a dozen cages are built into the hillside. North American animals. Further up the hill are the compounds where a single elk and a single buffalo try to roam. I think of setting them free, but it wouldn't do much good unless I had a horse van for them. Those who wear horns are the first ones to get shot. Three years ago the elk wasn't alone in her yard. There was a bull and three cows. A dead limb fell in a storm and knocked down the fence and the four of them got out. The bull was shot within an hour. It got close to the edge of the park and someone shot it with a telescopic rifle from one of the apartment buildings. A sportsman. By then the local police were on the scene and trying to herd the three cows back. One of them got too close to a cop who panicked and unloaded his gun into its neck. Another was hit by a city bus. The third one got back to its pen on its own. A fox or a coyote might still be able to run wild and survive in Sullivan Park, but not an animal with horns.

The Rodioners, the men chosen to be leaders by the Iroquois, they wore horns on their heads as a mark of the honor of that office. When Champlain came down the big lake into our land hundreds of years ago he fired his arquebus into a crowd of Iroquois people standing on the shore, watching his progress. Of those who were killed, several were men who wore horns. One of the reasons why we Swenogas stopped choosing chiefs — publicly, at least — was because of that. Because the ones who wear the horns get shot first. In the mid-1800's three Swenoga head chiefs in a row were shot by person or persons unknown soon after being elevated to their office. But Coyote doesn't wear horns and Coyote survives. We Swenogas usually learn by the third try. We stopped publicizing who our chiefs were.

"Okay, let's go around here."

"This isn't the bear cage."

"Have to start somewhere."

Peter opens the bolt cutter and grasps the padlock with it. He presses the handles towards each other and the metal shears like butter.

He whistles. "Nice!"

I swing the door open. A pair of small red shapes leap out and dart up the hill, their feet scrabbling the leaves.

"Good luck, Foxes," I say.

Peter is already cutting the lock on the next cage. He stands aside and I swing the door open. Nothing comes out.

"Coyote," I say, "you wouldn't trust your own grandfather, would you?" I can see him, a grey shape in the corner behind a paper maché log. I leave the door open. If we look back in five minutes, I know this cage, too, would be empty.

Between each of the cages is a narrow walkway. The one which leads to the door to the bear den deadends against the hillside. The den has been built against the rock cliff so that there is a cave in the rock itself, a place where a bear might hide. But the entrance to that cave is blocked off by a door which hasn't been opened in so long it's rusted shut. People who come to the zoo want to see the animals. The lock on the bear cage is twice as large as the others. From the rust on it it hasn't been opened for a long time. It takes Peter three tries to cut through it and even then the two of us have to wrestle with the lock to wedge it out.

My heart is beating fast and my arms feel weak. I'm about to turn the handle on the door to swing it open when I realize what I've been forgetting to remember. How are we going to get a four hundred pound black bear from a cage into a van a hundred yards away? Maybe, I think, if we back the van up to the alley between the cages, push the latch open with a long stick? I start to turn around to ask Peter what he thinks.

"You know. . ." I start to say, raising my hand as I turn. But my sleeve is caught on something. I jerk it hard and realize, just as I hear the click, that what my sleeve was caught on was the handle on the door. The door swings open then, slowly, as if something is pushing it. For a split second as I look up I see only darkness. My nose is filled with the heavy odor of a huge animal's piss and wet fur. I don't hear anything — not a growl or a roar — but then a heavy shape comes rolling out of the cage, right on top of me, crushing me to the ground.

II

You know, there's this theory I've got. Well, it isn't exactly mine. It's sort of one that Deskaheh had. He was the Cayuga who went to Europe to talk to the League of Nations about our people. He said the Little People were on good terms with us Iroquois because we got the Dark Dance. Whenever that ceremony takes place, the little ones come and dance with us. We hear their voices join in the singing and they feel real good about it, being thanked and included like that. That's what Deskaheh thought and I think so, too. The Cherokees and some of the others, they're scared of the Little People. All their stories about them, the Little People can't be trusted. Folks do something that gets the little folks angry and then they get hurt. Their little people are sort of treacherous from what I've heard. But us Long House People, we have the Dark Dance and so the Little People are friendly. That's what I believe. I've mentioned that to Foxy and he's said maybe that's why his people had it so hard. Because the Swenogas forgot to show respect to the Little People. *Mary,* he says, *maybe you got something there.* He's always interested in the old stories and that gets him hooked and he stays around for another cup of coffee or two — at least until he gets that look in his eye. Feels like he's about to be trapped or something, starts looking over his shoulder for the door. As if I was interested in an old dried-up thing like him anyhow. Gotta go, Mary, he says. Thanks for the coffee.

But I was talking about the Little People. There are places where we know they still live. You might not see as much of them as you did many years ago. I don't think they like the pollution any more than us Indians like it. They don't like all that noise that goes with the cities and the four-lane highways. So they make themselves scarce. You'd hardly know they were around most of the time — just like us Indians. But they haven't died off. Not by a long shot. I could show you this cave. And there's one ravine down by the creek where people who want to show the little folks that they're thinking about them still go and throw little bundles of fingernail clippings. The Little People like to use those clippings. I think it's that the scent of the human fingernails covers up their own scent when they go out hunting — or maybe it's to scare certain things off. Whatever it is, they like those nail clippings.

There's different tribes of them, you know. There's the Stone Throwers. They live on the cliffs and they aren't so friendly. You get too close to their territory and a rock will come whizzing at you and you'd better just turn around. Then there's the Underwater People. They have stone canoes that can come to the surface and then go underwater and they eat fish. Their faces are about as thin as a knife blade and they keep away from people. Sometimes you see little rolls and mounds of clay by the water's edge where they've been working making things. I've traveled out west some and Indian people there talk about water babies and I wonder if they might not be related.

Those little people who live by the streams, they don't like to have folks see them. There was this one place by the St. Ambrose river where they used to come — I heard this story from a Micmac — way up north. Anyhow, this one man decided he was going to watch them when they came out in the evening. He knew they wouldn't come out if they saw him, so he took his canoe down by the water, turned it over and hid underneath it. He told the people in the village he'd come back and tell them about what he saw. It came time for breakfast the next day and that man didn't come back. Then it was time for lunch and he still wasn't back. That was unusual, because that man really liked his meals.

When it came time for supper and he still wasn't back, his friends thought maybe he was staying to see the show for a second time. But when the next morning came and he didn't show up again for breakfast, they got a little worried. And when he wasn't there for lunch, they figured maybe they'd better go and look. They went down to the place where his canoe was by the water, but that canoe was turned right side up now. There was no sign of the man. There by the water, though, the clay had been piled up into a sort of a mound. They looked at that mound and saw it was shaped like a man. There were the arms and the legs and there, just in the middle of the head where the mouth would be, there was a little hole. The clay was all hard. They leaned close and they thought they could hear something like breathing come through that hole. So they broke the clay open and there was the man inside. He was just barely alive. They gave him water and got him up and he seemed to be okay, but he wouldn't talk about what happened to him. Not until he got back to the village. He told them that just when it got dark he was watching and watching. All of a sudden his canoe was turned over and he felt little hands all over him, pulling and pushing him. He didn't see anything, but the next thing he knew he was all covered over with clay and he couldn't move. So he never did see those little people, but he wasn't about to try again.

My favorite ones are the Little People who are in charge of the dew. They make sure that it gets on the flowers and the food plants. They specially love the strawberries and during the season when the strawberries are getting ripe they're the ones who turn the berries so that they ripen the same on all sides. Those are the Little People who keep a real close watch on things. One thing they do is see that stories aren't told during the summer. You start telling one of the old stories in the summer and a bee might fly right up and sting you to remind you it's the wrong time. That bee is one of the little ones in disguise. Or they might send snakes into your house. Storytelling time is after the first frost. They keep a close watch. On a lot of things. And I think they're keeping an even closer watch these days. Now that some people are finally waking up. That's what I believe.

There's also Little People whose job it is to guard the entrance to the underworld places where the really evil creatures are. Back when the world was new there were two boys, twins, born to the first woman who was born on earth. One of those twins was bad-minded and he made all kinds of dangerous creatures, monsters that would destroy the people. So his brother penned them up in caves under the earth and told the Little People to guard those places. Sometimes some of those evil things get out and the Little People have to round them up. It's a difficult job, protecting the world from evil things, you know that? And these days, those evil things are coming in all sorts of new shapes. But they still come from that same place. That's what I believe.

It took me a while to catch my breath. You'd take a while, too, if you were a man in his sixties who had four hundred pounds of black bear sprawled on top of you.

"Peter," I squeaked, "get me out from under this bear!"

From somewhere on the other side of the mountain of dark furry flesh which had rolled out onto me I heard Peter's voice.

"I'm trying, Foxy. He weighs a goddam ton!"

It took a bunch of pulling and pushing and prying, but somehow we got that bear rolled over enough for me to squeeze out from between it and the hillside. I had a few bruises, but that was all.

"What the hell did you do, Foxy? Hypnotize it?"

"You know as much as I do," I said. I leaned over and held my hand next to the bear's nose. "He's still breathing, but he's out cold. I guess he's knocked out from something those kids fed him, some kind of drugs."

"Is he dying?"

"I don't think so. Something tells me he's okay. But even if he's not, I think getting him out to the woods is the best thing. If he comes to, he'll be able to doctor himself out there."

We scouted around a little and found another tool shed with a heavy duty garden cart in it. The two of us managed to prop the bear up and roll him back into it. Lying on his back with his feet dangling, he looked like a kid out for a ride. We put down the ramp at the back of the van, rolled him up and dumped him in. While I put the garden cart back, Peter busied himself by the doors of the cages we'd opened. I came over to see what he was doing. With the awl point blade of his Swiss Army knife he was scratching a design into each of the doors. The shape of a bear paw. Not a bad idea. We checked to make sure the back of the van was closed up tight, started it up, and drove out of Sullivan Park.

Three Stories of Kayaderosseras

Down from the Adirondack foothills near the town of Corinth flows a small stream. It winds and widens as it passes through the towns of Wilton and Greenfield, Middle Grove, Rock City Falls and Ballston Spa. Finally it empties into Saratoga Lake. The old histories tell us the stream was named for its meandering path by the Iroquois. Caniaderossera, they called it: "The Crooked Stream." Its modern name is Kayaderosseras.

Two centuries ago, the wilderness was deep around Saratoga Springs. Even today, only two miles north of the modern racing city, there are thickly wooded places where a person can easily become lost. One such place is marked on topo maps with the name "Devil's Den." There the tangles of oak and raspberry and hop hornbeam pull at your clothing, trip your legs, turn you around back onto your own tracks. Though it has been logged over more than once and is bordered by roads — Daniels Road to the north, Braim Road to the west, North Greenfield Road and Old Route 9 on the two other sides, within that 20 square miles of brush and briar and second growth trees there are still no real trails. Autumn deer hunters keep to its edges or follow the powerline cut that angles one edge.

When my father was a boy running a trapline to feed his family during the Great Depression, he tracked a bobcat which had been caught in one of his traps and pulled free. He followed it to the edge of The Devil's Den, paused for a moment, then went in. The blood on the new snow and the drag mark of the metal trap made a trail which a sharp-eyed boy could follow. The day wore on, though, as he followed it. Before he knew it, it was late afternoon and the sun was disappearing below the treetops. He had to find his way out soon or spend the night in The Den. As my father tells the story, his few words only hint at what it was like. He doesn't mention the sounds one hears in that wilderness, that small part of what was once vast and deep-rooted, full of a spirit which was not human. Voices, perhaps, even in winter. Sounds which might be branches rubbed together by the wind or songs from a throat more ancient than most of us care to think much about. He went into The Devil's Den in the early morning. It was not until well after 9 at night that he reached a familiar road again. A year later, he said, as if that were the true end to his story, another man shot a bobcat with half of one front paw missing when his dogs cornered it behind his house on the Wilton Road. But there was no real end, for that small wilderness still remains, holding its stories, stories like the three which follow.

I
The Lost Hunter of Kayaderossera

Long ago, in the Hunting Moon, when only a few oak leaves still rattled in the wind and the first frost whitened the ground as the fat dripped from the Great Bear killed by the hunters in the sky, a young Mohawk hunter followed the crooked Kayaderosseras into those same woods. He had paddled upstream in his canoe and come upon the tracks of a moose. Leaving his canoe he followed the tracks for a long way until they disappeared on rocky ground. Then, looking about, he realized he had lost his way. Though he was a good hunter, he became confused. The wildness of the place overcame him and he began to wander like a child, going in circles, cutting his own trail again and again as he went. He felt that some strong medicine was working against him. The circles he was making would become smaller and smaller until, at their center, he would meet something which would be an embodiment of this spot: indifferent and awful. He tried to find a way out, but one day wore into the next. The sun did not show through the thick grey cloud and he came to his own tracks time and again. Now he had eaten all of his pemmican and he still saw no game to hunt, though he kept his bow and arrows and knife.

At last, as the fourth day of his wandering was drawing to a close, just as the last faint light was fading from the pale sky, he came to a small clearing. Something large flew in front of him, almost touching his face with its big wings. He fell to the ground to avoid it. It flapped across the clearing and glided noiselessly to rest on the bare limb of an old hemlock broken by lightning. It was a great grey owl. Its eyes were like twin moons. They stared into his eyes and he knew this was an evil spirit. It seemed to speak to him as he looked into its eyes and he felt his feet begin to move across the clearing towards the blasted tree.

But he was a man born of the flint. He forced his feet to stop, lifted up his bow, put an arrow to the string and let it fly. The arrow struck the owl. It let out a terrible cry, like that of a human being in agony, and fell off the limb.

The Mohawk hunter ran up to it, ready to strike a final blow. But before he could reach it a white bird flew up in front of him. It seemed as if it came from the place where the owl had fallen. As it spread its wings above him the storm clouds cleared from the sky and the gentle light of Grandmother Moon filled the forest. The bird flew away, heading towards the west. The hunter followed. He walked through the night. When the sun rose at his back he found himself again on the shores of the stream, his elmbark canoe where he had left it concealed, weighted down with stones just beneath the surface. He floated downstream until he came to the Saratoga Lake, followed its shore to the Creek of Many Fish and then down to the great river, the Hudson. When he reached the lodges of his people, he had a new story to tell them, the story of the lost hunter who was saved by the White Spirit Bird of Kayaderossera.

II
The Mourning Kill

A brook rises near what is now the town of Galway. It flows down through farmlands and wild meadows, bends northward near the town of Ballston Spa and then joins the Kayaderosseras at a point halfway between the Delaware and Hudson railroad tracks and the elevation of Malta Ridge to the east. Part of the old war trail which led from north to south crossed those streams as the Mohawks and the Adirondacks contested control of these rich lands for hunting, trapping, fishing and the growing of corn.

It was the Moon When the Wild Roses Blossom. A band of Mohawk hunters were making the carry from Ballston Lake to the Kayaderosseras, following the banks of the Mourning Kill where the roses were white with bloom. They met, coming from the north, a band of Adirondacks. The Sun was just rising and if it is true that the Sun loves the sounds and sights of war — as the Iroquois people say — then it looked down with pleasure on the battle which began. Arrows flew and war clubs fell. A war eagle flew down above the fighting men. Both sides looked up at the bird, claimed it as an omen of their coming victory, and then fought harder.

But the men on both sides were brave and their two bands equal in strength. The grass of the meadow was trampled down and men closed their eyes for the last time, but neither side could overcome the other. War cries echoed across the wild meadow, answered by the screams of the eagle circling low overhead. The white roses turned red from the blood of men. They are red to this day along those banks.

At last, just as the sun began to set, there was a pause in the battle. Even the eagle seemed to grow tired. It swooped down to land on the limb of a broken pine tree above the stream, folded its wings, and stared at the men below. Both the Mohawks and the Adirondacks looked at the eagle. They had seen this bird as a sign of their victory, but was it that? Neither side was close to defeating the other, though much blood had been shed. This bird was friend to neither side. It had only made them more eager to kill each other. All of the men who still survived felt angry and betrayed. They drew back their bows and many arrows flew through the air, striking the eagle from its perch.

As soon as its body struck the ground, though, a white bird flew up — as if from the eagle's breast. It was the Spirit Bird of Kayaderossera and its message to both sides was the message of peace. It flew up and away towards the west, disappearing into the sunset. Then both Mohawk and Adirondack put away their weapons. Together they buried their dead and cared for each other's wounds. They called each other brother and vowed the place would always be a place of peace.

For many years thereafter in the Moon When the Roses Bloom the men of both nations returned to the scene of their battle, one generation following the next. They met at the meadow where the roses were still red as the blood of brave men, spoke of the old days, shared food and remembered those who died there before they listened to the message of peace from the Spirit Bird at the place which they called the Stream of Mourning, The Mourning Kill.

III

The Spirits of Lake Tassawassa

An Indian Story of Yaddo

Long ago, the story goes, Mohican people came north each summer to camp on the hill above a small creek which ran down into the Great Bear Swamp and the Kayaderosseras. The Mohawks also claimed that land, but the two peoples kept a sort of peace. Because that small springfed stream which rose in a ravine reminded them of the Tassawassa Creek in their winter home, south in the Taghankick Mountains, the Mohicans referred to the brook by that same name — Tassawassa. Where the ravine broadened to the north of the high knoll beavers had built a dam and formed a small lake. The Mohicans called that lake, too, Tassawassa.

Years passed, and the Mohawks and Mohicans began to quarrel over the land of Kayaderossera. The Europeans had come and the British and French in particular were struggling over control of the new continent. Both sides were paying high prices for beaver skins and the competition for furs and for control of good lands for trapping the beaver was fierce. Soon the beaver were wiped out in first one area and then another and there was fighting. For a long time the area in and around Tassawassa was a place of peace. Tassawassa was not far from the Medicine Spring of the Great Spirit, a powerful healing place, and it was a long tradition that the people would pass through the area in peace. So it was that a small band of Mohicans still dared to return each year to the hill above Lake Tassawassa and build their summer lodges on the hill which faced east towards The Silent Lake, now known as Lake Saratoga.

It is said that the old sachem of those Mohican people was named Wewanis and he brought with him his only child, a daughter. Her name was Awonunsk. It is said, also, that there was a young man, a good hunter, who fell in love with Awonunsk. His name was Wekwagun. The old sachem approved of this young hunter and made no move to interfere on the evenings when Wekwagun stood in the trees outside their lodge and played a courting song on a flute made of cedar.

Awonunsk walked outside those nights — to get water from the stream, she said — and Wewanis smiled, remembering his own younger days. It was soon decided that the two young people would formally begin their life together during the Moon of Wild Strawberries.

The wild strawberries grew in profusion in the meadow on the other side of Lake Tassawassa, just at the edge of Great Bear Swamp. On the day before their marriage, Awonunsk went with some of her friends to gather strawberries. They crossed the lake in their canoes and carried their baskets to the meadow where berries glowed red as the embers of a fire. No sooner had they begun to fill their baskets than Awonunsk thought she saw movement in the tall grass. "What is that?" she said, pointing with her lips towards the motion as she stopped picking berries. A wild howl, like that of a hunting wolf, split the air. It was a Mohawk war cry. A dozen Mohawk warriors came running out of the swamp where they had been hidden, moving to cut off the women. Only Awonunsk, the fastest of the young women, escaped capture. She ran across the meadow and reached the side of the lake. Leaping into her canoe, she paddled it out into the water with a few quick strokes. The leader of the Mohawk war party was close behind her, though. He jumped into another of the canoes and pushed out from the shore.

On the other side, some Mohican men had heard Awonunsk's cries for help and came down to the water's edge. All their canoes were on the other side, but they shouted encouragement as they watched. It seemed certain that Awonunsk would escape, for she was drawing close to the safety of the shore. The Mohawk war leader, though, enraged by the thought of his prey escaping him, raised his own bow and fired an arrow. It struck Awonunsk in the back. She raised her arms towards the shore she would never reach, towards her husband-to-be, Wekwagun. Then she fell from the canoe into the lake.

The Mohawk war leader immediately tried to turn his own canoe and escape, but the father of Awonunsk was too quick for him. Wewawis pulled back the string of his own bow and let go. An arrow pierced the throat of the Mohawk. He, too, fell into the clear waters of Tassawassa, no more than a heartbeat after Awonunsk. The blood of the two stained the lake and the sky above darkened with clouds.

The Mohicans tried to recapture the women, but the Mohawk war party escaped. They tried to find the body of Awonunsk, but it was lost beneath the surface of the lake whose once clean waters were now murky and forbidding. The sky remained dark as the waters and thick mists formed. It was that omen of ill-fortune as much as the fear of the return of an even larger war party of Mohawks which led the Mohicans to decide they must leave their hill above the lake.

The years that followed saw much warfare in the lands around Lake Tassawassa. Its shores remained uninhabited and the cloud above the lake hung there day and night, the black waters reflecting the black sky, the strange mists as thick as smoke. Nothing grew there and the lake was empty of life as the land. No one dared come near that cursed place except for one man and a few of his friends. Each summer, during the Moon of Wild Strawberries, Wekwagun would return to the place where Awonunsk died. He would look out over the lake and see within the ever-present mists Awonunsk struck by the fatal arrow, lifting her arms, falling into the water. He would stand there for a time, then turn without speaking and return south, followed by the few friends who came with him out of respect for his courage and his devotion.

More years went by and now Wekwagun grew old. He made his pilgrimages to Tassawassa with the help of younger men now, for all his friends had walked up the Great Road of the Milky Way to join the old people in the Sky Land. At last a year came when the young men were sure that the old man would die before reaching the lake. However, though his steps were feeble, he was determined. At last he came to the spot which, with its dark cloud, strange mists, and black water, was frightening to the young men. He stood on the shore of the lake and looked once more into the mists, expecting to see for a final time, the death of the woman he loved. But a strange thing happened then. He saw, instead of that last futile flight, Awonunsk herself. She stood on the water before him, her face bright and calm. When asked later what they saw, the young men who accompanied the old man said that their eyes were almost blinded by a strange light that opened the mists.

Wekwagun held out his arms. "My wife," he said, "I am ready to go with you." Then he fell dead on the shore. At that moment, the dark clouds above parted and the sun shone through. The young men who had come with Wekwagun looked at the lake and saw not one bright light now, but two. It was the spirit forms of Wekwagun and Awonunsk, together at last. As the young men watched, the lights lifted up into the sky, following the spirit trail to the place where the berries are always ripe and the hunting is good forever. And the waters of Lake Tassawassa again were clear.

So, they say, the clouds were lifted long ago from the shores of Lake Tassawassa in the place now called Yaddo. Perhaps, if you walk in the valley of the small stream where four small lakes glitter under a summer sun, you may feel as if you are not alone. Perhaps it is the presence of a faithful man and the woman he loved, two whose spirits were stronger than death.

Turtle Meat

"Old Man, come in. I need you."

The old woman's cracked voice carried out to the woodshed near the overgrown field. Once it had been planted with corn and beans, the whole two acres. But now mustard heads rolled in the wind and wild carrot bobbed among nettles and the blue flowers of thistles. *A goat would like to eat those thistles,* Homer LaWare thought. *Too bad I'm too old to keep a goat.* He put down the ax handle he had been carving, cast one quick look at the old bamboo fishing pole hanging over the door and then stood up.

"Coming over," he called out. With slow careful steps he crossed the fifty yards between his shed and the single-story house with the picture window and the gold-painted steps. He swung open the screen door and stepped over the dishes full of dog food. *Always in front of the door,* he thought.

"Where?" he called from the front room.

"Back here, I'm in the bathroom. I can't get up."

He walked as quickly as he could through the cluttered kitchen. The breakfast dishes were still on the table. He pushed open the bathroom door. Mollie was sitting on the toilet.

"Amalia Wind, what's wrong?" he said.

"My legs seem to of locked, Homer. Please just help me to get up. I've been hearing the dogs yapping for me outside the door and the poor dears couldn't even get to me. Just help me up."

He slipped his hand under her elbow and lifted her gently. He could see that the pressure of his fingers on the white wrinkled flesh of her arm was going to leave marks. She'd always been like that. She always bruised easy. But it hadn't stopped her from coming for him . . . and getting him. It hadn't stopped her from throwing Jake Wind out of her house and bringing Homer LaWare to her farm to be the hired man.

Her legs were unsteady for a few seconds but then she seemed to be all right. He removed his arms from her.

"Just don't know how it happened, Homer. I ain't so old as that, am I, Old Man?"

"No, Amalia. That must of was just a cramp. Nothing more than that."

They were still standing in the bathroom. Her long grey dress had fallen down to cover her legs but her underpants were still around her ankles. He felt awkward. Even after all these years, he felt awkward.

"Old Man, you just get out and do what you were doing. A woman has to have her privacy. Get now."

"You sure?"

"Sure? My Lord! If I wasn't sure do you think I'd have any truck with men like you?" She poked him in the ribs. "You know what you should do, Old Man? You should go down to that pond and do that fishing you said you were going to do."

He didn't want to leave her alone, but he didn't want to tell her that. And there was something in him that urged him towards that pond where the yellow perch had been biting for the last few days according to Jack Crandall. Jack had told him that when he brought his ax by to have Homer fit a new handle.

"I still got Jack's ax to fix, Amalia."

"And when did it ever take you more than a minute to fit a handle into anything, Old Man?" There was a wicked gleam in her eye. For a few seconds she looked forty years younger in the old man's eyes.

He shook his head.

"Miss Wind, I swear those ladies was right when they said you was going to hell." She made a playful threatening motion with her hand and he backed out the door. "But I'm going."

It took him another hour to finish carving the handle to the right size. It slid into the head like a hand going into a velvet glove. His hands shook when he started the steel wedge that would hold it in tight, but it took only three strokes with the maul to put the wedge in. He looked at his hands, remembering the things they'd done. Holding the reins of the last horse they'd had on the farm — twenty years ago. Or was it thirty. Lifting the sheets back from Mollie's white body that first night. Swinging in tight fists at the face of Jake Wind the night he came back, drunk and with a loaded .45 in his hand. He'd gone down hard and Homer had emptied the shells out of the gun and broken its barrel with his maul on his anvil. Though Jake had babbled of the law that night, neither the law nor Jake ever came back to the Wind farm. It had been Amalia's all along. Her father'd owned it and Jake had married her for it. She'd never put her property in any man's name, never would. That was what she always said.

"I'm not asking, Amalia." That was what Homer said to her after the first time together in her brass bed, just before he dressed and went back to sleep the rest of the night away in his cot in the shed. He always slept there. All the years. "I'm not asking for any property, Amalia. It's the Indian in me don't want to own no land."

That was Homer's favorite saying. Whenever there was something about him that seemed maybe different from what others expected he would say simply, "It's the Indian in me." Sometimes he thought of it not just as a part of him but as another man, a man with a name he didn't know but would recognize if he heard it.

His father had said that phrase often. His father had come down from Quebec and spoke French and, sometimes, to his first wife who died when Homer was six, another language that Homer never heard again after her death. His father had been a quiet man who made baskets from the ash trees that grew on their farm. "But he never carried them into town," Homer said with pride. "He just stayed on the farm and let people come to him if they wanted to buy them."

The farm had gone to a younger brother who sold out and moved west. There had been two other children. None of them got a thing, except Homer who got his father's best horse. In those early years Homer worked for Seneca Smith at his mill. Woods work, two-man saws and sledding the logs out in the snow. He did it until his thirtieth year when Amalia asked him to come and work at her farm. Though people talked, he had done it. When anyone asked him why he let himself be run by a woman that way he said, in the same quiet voice his father used, "It's the Indian in me."

The pond was looking glass smooth. Homer stood beside the boat. Jack Crandall had given him the key to unlock the chain that held it to the dock. Homer looked into the water. He saw his face, the skin lined and brown as an old map. Wattles of flesh hung below his chin like a rooster's.

"Damn, you are a good-looking man, Homer LaWare," he said to his reflection. "Easy to see what a woman sees in you." He thought again of Mollie seated in the rocker and looking out the picture window. As he left he heard her old voice calling the names of the small dogs she loved so much. *Those dogs were the only one ever give back her love,* he thought, *not that no-good daughter. Last time she come was in Christmas in '68 to give her that pissy green second-hand shawl and try to run me off again.*

Homer stepped into the boat. Ripples wiped his face from the surface of the pond. He put his bamboo pole and the can of worms down in front of him and levered the oars into the locks, one at a time, breathing hard as he did so. He pulled the anchor rope into the boat and looked out across the water. A brown stick projected above the water in the middle of the pond. *Least it looks like a stick, but if it moves . . .* The stick moved, slid across the surface of the pond for a few feet and then disappeared. Homer watched with narrowed eyes until it reappeared a hundred feet further out. It was a turtle, a snapping turtle. Probably a big one.

"I see you out there, Turtle," Homer said. "Maybe you and me are going to see more of each other."

He felt in his pocket for the familiar shape of his bone-handled knife. He pushed the red handkerchief that held it deep in the pocket more firmly into place. Then he began to row. In the middle of the pond he stopped. It was time to begin to fish. The baited hook plopped into the water. Within a few minutes the fish started to hit. He pulled them in as fast as he could bait up. Yellow-stomached perch with bulging dark eyes. Most were about a foot long. When he had thirteen he stopped, leaving the baited line in the water. He pulled out the bone-handled knife and opened it. The blade was thin as the handle of a spoon from thirty years of sharpening. It was like a razor. Homer always carried a sharp knife. He made a careful slit from the ventral opening of the fish up to its gills and spilled the guts into the water, leaning over the side of the boat. He talked as he cleaned the fish.

"Old Knife, you cut good," he said. He had cleaned nearly every fish now, hardly wasting a movement. Almost as fast as when he was a boy. *Some things don't go from you so . . .*

The jerking of his pole brought him back from his thoughts. It was being dragged overboard. He dropped the knife, grabbed the pole as it went over. He pulled up and the pole bent almost double. *No fish pulls like that.* It was the turtle. He began reeling the line in, slow and steady so it wouldn't break. Soon he saw it, wagging its head back and forth, coming up from the green depths of the pond where it had been gorging on the perch guts and grabbed his hook.

"Come up and talk, Turtle," Homer said.

The turtle opened its mouth as if to say something and the hook slipped out, the pole jerking back in Homer's hands. *Jaw's too tough for a hook to stick in. Now it's going to swim away.* But the turtle stayed there, just under the surface. *Big. Thirty pounds or more.* It was looking for more food. Homer put another worm on the hook with trembling hands and dropped it in front of the turtle's mouth.

"Turtle, you want this one, too."

Homer could see the wrinkled skin under its throat as it turned its head to look, eyes patterned like stars. A leech of some kind was on the back of its head, another hanging from its right front leg. It was an old turtle. Skin rough, shell green with algae. It grabbed the hook with one lazy sideways turn of its head. As Homer pulled up to snag the hook in its mouth, the turtle reached forward with its front feet and grabbed the line like a man grasping a rope to climb it. Its front claws looked as long as the teeth of a bear.

Homer pulled up hard. The turtle held the hook in its mouth and rose to the surface. It was strong and the old man wondered if he could hold it up. Did he want turtle meat that much? But he didn't slack off on the line. The turtle was next to the boat and the hook only holding because of the pressure on the line. A little slack and it would be gone. Homer put the butt of his pole under his leg, grabbing with the freed hand for the anchor rope. He fastened a noose in it as the turtle shook its head, moving the twelve-foot boat as it struggled. Homer could smell it now. Its heavy musk was everywhere. It wasn't a good smell or a bad smell. It was the smell of the turtle.

Now the noose was ready. He hung it over the side. Time for the hard part now, the part that would have been easy when his arms were young and his chest wasn't caved in like a broken box. He let go of the pole and reached down fast, grabbed the turtle's tail with his left hand and pulled. The turtle came out of the water, back legs against the boat. The boat almost tipped over, but Homer kept his balance. The turtle swung its big head, mouth open wide enough to swallow a softball. It hissed like a snake, ready to grab hard at anything in reach. Gasping as he did it, feeling the turtle's rough tail slipping, tearing the palm of his left hand, Homer swung the noose in his right hand up around the turtle's neck. Its weight pulled the slip knot tight just as the turtle's jaws clamped tight with a snap on Homer's sleeve.

"Turtle, I believe I got you and you got me," Homer said. He slipped a turn of the rope around his left foot with his free arm. He pulled back to free his sleeve from the turtle's jaws, but it did not let go. "I understand you, Turtle," Homer said, "you don't like to let go." He breathed hard, closed his eyes for a moment until the pounding in his temples went away. Then Homer took the knife in his left hand. He leaned over and slid it across the turtle's neck. Dark fluid pulsed out into the water, spread under the surface like blossoms opening. A hissing noise came from between the turtle's clenched jaws, but it held onto the old man's sleeve. The blood came out for a long time, but the turtle still held on. At last Homer took the knife and cut off the end of his sleeve, leaving it in the turtle's mouth.

He sat up straight in the boat for the first time since he had hooked the turtle. He looked around. It was dark. He could hardly see the shore. He had been fighting the turtle for longer than he thought.

By the time he reached the shore and docked the sounds of the turtle banging against the side of the boat had stopped. He couldn't tell if blood was still flowing from its cut throat. Night had turned all of the water that same dark shade. He couldn't find the perch in the bottom of the boat. It didn't matter. The raccoons could have them. He had his knife and his pole and the turtle. He dragged it up to his old Ford truck. It was too heavy to carry.

There were cars parked in the driveway when he pulled in. He had to park behind his shed, near the small mounds each marked with a wooden cross and a neatly lettered name. He heard voices as he walked up through the darkness.

"Old fool's finally come back," a voice said. A voice rough as a rusted hinge. Molly's daughter.

He pushed the door open. "Where's Amalia?" he said. Someone screamed. The room was full of faces and they were all looking at him.

"Ole bastard looks like he scalped someone," a pock-faced man with a grey crewcut muttered.

Homer looked at himself in the light. His arms and hands were dark with the blood of the turtle. His right sleeve was tattered. His trousers were muddy. His fly half open. He straightened his back. "Where's Amalia," he demanded.

"What the hell you been up to, you ole fart?" said the raspy voiced daughter. He turned to look hard into her loose-featured face. She was sitting in Molly's rocker.

"I been fishin'."

The daughter stood up. Jake Wind was written all over her face, carved into her bones.

"You wanna know where Moms is, huh? Wanna know where your ole sweetheart's gone to? Well, I'll tell you. We got her sent off to a place that'll take care of her, even if she is cracked. Come in to find her sittin' talkin' to dogs been dead and gone for years. Dishes full of dog food for ghosts. Maybe you better eat some of it because your meal ticket's been canceled, you old bastard. This man here is a doctor and he's decided my dear mother was mentally incompetent. The ambulance to the Home took her out of here half an hour ago."

She kept talking, saying things she must have longed to say for years. Homer LaWare was not listening. His eyes slowly took in and held onto the details of the room he had walked through every day for the last forty-seven years. Furniture he had mended when it broke, the picture window he had installed, the steps he had painted every spring, the neatly stacked dishes from which he had eaten his food three times each day for almost half a century. The daughter was still talking, talking as if this was a scene she had rehearsed for many years, talking louder now. She was screaming. Homer LaWare hardly heard her. He closed his eyes, remembering how the turtle held onto his sleeve, even after its breath was cut and its life leaking out into the dark pond.

The screaming stopped. He opened his eyes and saw that the man with the grey crew-cut hair was holding the daughter's arms. She had a plate in her hands. Maybe she had been about to hit him. Homer looked at her. It didn't matter. He looked at the other people in the room. They seemed to be waiting for him to speak.

"I got a turtle to clean," he said, knowing what it was in him that spoke. Then he turned and walked into the darkness.

Acknowledgements

"Going Home" was the winner of a 1983 PEN Syndicated Fiction Award. It appeared in newspapers in San Francisco and Minneapolis and in *The Available Press/PEN Short Story Collection.*

"The Ice-Hearts" was published in 1979 as a chapbook by Cold Mountain Press.

"Jed's Grandfather" first appeared in *Blueline.*

"The Fox Den" first appeared in *Groundswell.*

"Turtle Meat" was first published in *Earth Power Coming,* Edited by Simon Ortiz, Navajo Community College Press.

"Code Talkers" won the 1986 Cherokee Nation Prose Award and appeared in *The Phoenix.*

"The White Moose" and *"All Dishonest Men"* were published in a chapbook, *The White Moose,* by *Blue Cloud Quarterly.*

"The Trout" first appeared in *Combinations.*

"Mayor Schuyler and the Mohican" first appeared in *Gates to the City,* the Albany Bicentennial anthology.

"How Mink Stole Time" was published in *Parabola.*

Special Thanks to the Corporation of Yaddo for a Residency Fellowship which enabled me to complete a number of these stories.

Joseph Bruchac lives with his wife, Carol in the same house in the Adirondack foothills where he was raised by his grandparents. They have two grown sons. Much of Joseph's writing draws on that land and the Abenaki heritage on the maternal side of his family. Although his Indian heritage is only part of an ethnic background that includes Slovak and English blood, those Native roots are the deepest ones in this soil and he has tended and watered them the most. From 1966 to 1969 he lived and taught in Ghana, West Africa and on his return to the United States founded the Greenfield Review Press. Co-author with Michael Caduto of *Keepers of the Earth,* Joseph Bruchac's poems, articles and stories have appeared in many publications, from *Akwesasne Notes* and *American Poetry Review* to *National Geographic* and *Parabola.* As a professional teller of the traditional tales of the Adirondacks and the native peoples of the Northeastern Woodlands, he has performed in Europe and throughout the United States. Although his prose has enjoyed some critical success, including a PEN Syndicated Fiction Award, *Turtle Meat* is the first published collection of his original short stories.

Murv Jacob is a painter/pipemaker who lives and works in Tahlequah, Oklahoma. Descended from the Kentucky Cherokees, Jacob is noted for his intricate, brightly-colored, meticulously researched paintings which have won him numerous awards. His cover art appears on publications from Doubleday, Beacon Press, The University of Oklahoma Press and Parabola Books.